Beyond Cutting Edge

A journey of
Grief, Grace and Healing

Biblical
BOOKS

BY AVERIL NEILLY WITH VICTOR MAXWELL

Beyond the Cutting Edge

A Journey of Grief, Grace and Healing
By Averil Neilly with Victor Maxwell

©Averil Neilly & Victor Maxwell 2013

Printed by JC Print Limited
Email: info@jcprint.net

Beyond The Cutting Edge

I dedicate this book to my three wonderful children, Hannah, Matthew and Samuel.

"I have no greater joy than to hear that my children walk in truth"
(3 John 4).

Contents

	Foreword	9
1	Grief and Pain	11
2	Wiping Tears and Giving Thanks	20
3	Reliving Our Dream	29
4	Tyrone Among the Bushes	34
5	A Son of the Manse	42
6	Between Church and University	51
7	The Blending	63
8	On the Way to the Altar	70
9	Making Roots	77
10	Mountains and Valleys	88
	Photographic Section *between 96 & 97*	
11	A Deep Trough	97
12	The Last Lap	106
13	Friends Indeed	113
14	Where is God's Answer?	123
15	Samuel Makes Me Smile	129
16	Hallelujah for Hannah	133
17	Meet Matthew	141
18	How Dark is Your Valley?	151
19	Grace for the Grief	158
20	Helpful Tokens	166
	Postscript	170

Acknowledgements

I was the wife of Paul Neilly, Consultant Surgeon at Altnagelvin Hospital.

I want to say a very sincere thank you to all who helped me in writing this book by recalling their memories of Paul. They have been a tremendous help.

Very special thanks to Victor Maxwell for motivating me to write and for his unending patience with me throughout the process.

Thanks to Joe and Roberta Costley for guidance and decision making in regard to finished article.

A big thank-you to my children for putting pen to paper to record their deepest sentiment about their dad. It certainly was not easy for them.

I am grateful to my heavenly Father for sustaining me as I endeavoured to share my heart with others who may read this book and find themselves in a very similar situation. May God bless and help them as He has helped me.

Thank you,

Averil

Foreword

When Paul and Averil Neilly and their three children began attending Ballycraigy Congregational Church, where I was the minister, I soon discovered that God had sent us a special family. The longer they were with us the more special they became as they endeared themselves to our entire congregation. Their presence among us and their contribution to the life and work of the church were exceptional.

When we learned that Paul was seriously ill, especially with the form of cancer in which he, as a surgeon, specialised, we were filled with total disbelief but, sadly, it was true.

I had been their pastor in times of health and success and now I was trying to be a pastor to a young, highly skilled surgeon, husband and father who was terminally ill.

It is virtually impossible for me to describe how this remarkable couple faced such an unexpected situation as they displayed such a spirit of grace, dignity and trust in God.

Probably I will never again meet a wife who revealed the strength and spirit of God in such devastating circumstances as Averil. No doubt they had their low times, but I was often amazed at her resilience as she constantly attended to Paul's needs.

I am delighted that this story is being told because it is a record of God's faithfulness in human lives in the midst of severe trial and testing and a testimony of real grace in lives totally committed to God, whatever the cost.

May God make this book a great blessing and a deep challenge to all who read it.

Tom Shaw

Chapter 1

Grief and Pain

On the morning of the 18th February 2004, I opened our bedroom curtains and looked out onto a very bleak and dismal world. It was the first day after my husband's funeral, my first day as a widow. Not only was it damp and cold, but low clouds hung heavily over Limavady as drizzling rain soaked the murky landscape. However, the dull and depressing scene on the outside only reflected and heightened how I was feeling on the inside. I was numb, not with the cold and clouds of that sombre morning, but stunned with deep and inexpressible grief and unrelenting heartache. My whole outlook seemed to be shrouded in the darkest possible grey.

In this thickening fog of sorrow I was thinking of my three precious children downstairs and how they had been deprived of their daddy. I did not want to be here any more. I longed to be where my husband, Paul, had just gone. I wakened that morning to the stark realisation that he was no longer with us. I could no longer go to Paul, touch him, care for him or hug him.

I had known for some months that Paul was going to die,

but no matter how often I saw him in the hospice, I had never really been able to envisage my life without him by my side. The end of Paul's life was like a song that had been suddenly cut off while the refrain continued in my mind, or like a tale, which had only been half told, and I was longing for the rest of the story.

I felt it was so ironic that Paul had passed away on the day after Valentine's Day. During the previous fourteen years Paul had never failed to present me with a lovely arrangement of roses and a meaningful card, and he always organised for us to have a romantic meal on that special date.

However, on that Saturday morning, 14th February 2004, while I was driving from Limavady to the Foyle Hospice in Londonderry all sorts of thoughts kept swimming round my head. How different this day was from all the other Valentine Days we had enjoyed together. This year there would be no affectionate card, no colourful flowers or starry-eyed meal. Although he remained lucid in his mind, due to the deterioration of his condition, Paul's coordination was poor. For that reason, writing a Valentine card would be out of the question for him, and any stars in my eyes had long since been replaced by salty tears coursing down my cheeks.

As we neared Londonderry I quickly tore my thoughts away from Valentine's Day to the little boy sitting in the passenger seat nervously clutching an unopened brown envelope. Our son, Matthew, had just received his 11+ examination results in the mail. The outcome of that examination would determine if he had gained an entrance into grammar school or not. He clutched the still unopened envelope as he sat at my side. He had purposely refused to open it until he could do so at his daddy's bedside in the hospice. Although Matthew's gesture was very touching, at the same time it was causing me a great deal of anxiety in case he had not achieved the desired results.

For me it was even more moving as I watched Matthew excitedly meet his dad, then hurriedly open the envelope and announce to us that he had been successful in his school transfer exam. There were spontaneous tears of joy shed as father and son hugged each other.

I was taken aback when Paul then indicated to me that I also had an envelope to open. It was a Valentine's card. Paul, with the help of his younger brother, Mark, had managed to write a few words about his love for me inside the card. This loving token proved Paul's deep love and devotion to me and our children in the face of impending death. Before we had to leave the hospice I lingered a few moments longer to be alone with Paul. I kissed him goodbye and thanked him for the beautiful card. In spite of his extreme weakness he managed to tell me that he loved me. I tried to restrain my tears until I had left his room.

Later that same afternoon I got an urgent telephone call asking me to return to the hospice as Paul had been asking for me. Fortunately, I was able to drop all and go back to Londonderry immediately as Paul's parents had been staying with us in our Limavady home during the previous few weeks.

On arrival at his bedside I found that Paul was very agitated. However, when he became aware that I was with him he settled a little and became more restful and calm. I asked the nursing staff if I would be able to stay at the hospice that night in case Paul should need me again. The carers were always most attentive to the needs of their patients and the requests of their visiting families, and they gladly made a room available for me.

Many visitors called by the hospice that evening. These included members of our families, elders from our church in Limavady and Rev Tom Shaw. Paul's brother, Mark, and his wife, Hazel, asked if they could stay overnight with us at the hospice. I was glad to have their support.

During that night the three of us alternated between sitting on recliner chairs at Paul's bedside or resting in the room that had been allocated to us. We were glad that Paul had a very peaceful night.

Early next morning Paul was still in a deep sleep and seemed to be without any pain or discomfort. Nevertheless, I kept vigil at his bedside in case he should waken. I should say that at no point during all the time he was at the Foyle Hospice, did I ever visit Paul and find him in physical pain.

Several hours later that morning, content that Paul continued to sleep peacefully, I went to the kitchen to make some tea and toast while Mark and Hazel stayed with Paul. I had little or no appetite. Even though this was the case, I think that I must have indulged a little in comfort eating.

While I was still in the hospice kitchen one of the nurses suddenly burst in to tell me that Paul's condition had suddenly changed for the worse and that he was deteriorating quite rapidly. I left everything and immediately rushed back to Paul's bedside to spend my last moments with my darling husband. Mark and Hazel were still in Paul's room, but at a distance from the bedside.

News of Paul's worsening condition was quickly communicated to our families and soon they were on their way to the hospice. The nurses reserved a room aside for them, supplied tea and coffee while they waited with me until Paul had passed away.

I clung to the side of Paul's bed. Although he did not seem to be conscious I told him how much I loved him and assured him that we would meet again in heaven. I could not be certain that he heard me or knew what I was saying, but I never left his bedside. I held my husband's soft hand until he finally left us at about 1.00pm. Without a whisper he quietly departed from the Foyle Hospice to go to meet his Saviour and be at home in the Father's house as Jesus Christ had promised. It was all over so quickly and, thankfully, so peacefully.

Although Paul had gone I lingered on by his bedside while other close family members came in to comfort me and mourn Paul's passing. It was a surreal moment. Paul's still form could not respond to our comments or tears.

While driving home later, all I could think of was how I was going to tell the children. A strange sensation came over me and the finality of my husband's death seemed to dry up my tears. It began to dawn on me that it was all over. Paul was finally at rest. This was not the time for tears. I needed to be composed so that I would be able to tell the children that their dad had slept away.

Although other family members were at our house when I arrived, I took Hannah, Matthew and Samuel with me into the drawing room. As best I could I told them that their daddy had passed away peacefully and he was now in heaven with the Lord Jesus. Even though Paul and I had tried to prepare our children for this day, it still was heart breaking for them to hear this sorry news. Each of them reacted differently. As they wept I did my best to reassure them. Paul always had our children's needs uppermost in his mind, especially during his time in the hospice. Now that he was gone I promised them I would try to do my best and with God's help, I would always be there for them. Now, looking back over the years, my hope and prayer is that I have made the right decisions for our three children in Paul's absence.

Prior to his death Paul had expressed his desire for his remains to be kept at the funeral home. He did not want our children to have memories of seeing their dad lying in a casket in our home. Furthermore, he had always been a very private and dignified person, and therefore, had asked me to ensure that his coffin was kept closed. Paul did not want a lot of idle comments made about his appearance after his demise. We complied with his wishes, although his body remained overnight at the Foyle Hospice before it was transferred to the funeral home in Limavady on the following day.

During the three-day wake, even though our Limavady home was private, the house was constantly busy with a steady stream of many family members, friends, ministers and undertakers coming to sympathise and support us. I knew that these were people who cared for us deeply. I tried to make everyone's visit as pleasant as possible.

Perhaps it was this busyness in the home that in a strange way gave me the illusory impression that Paul was still present with us while I was entertaining his friends. The finality of his death had not yet set in. I had already read a little about grief and this seemed to be a period where we were carried along by the prayers of many friends. It was a very bizarre experience. I was surprised that I could be so sufficiently composed to be able to discuss the funeral plans with the undertaker and Pastor Jim Smyth, our former pastor at Limavady Baptist Church. I even tried to comfort others who came to visit our home.

Paul and I had already agreed that at the funeral all donations given in lieu of flowers would be divided between the Child Evangelism Fellowship's Wonder Book and the Foyle Hospice.

On the evening prior to the funeral, our daughter, Hannah, pleaded with me not to make her attend the funeral service at the church. She could not bear the thought of looking at the casket containing her father's remains. Hannah was merely twelve years old. Our youngest child, Samuel, who was only eight years old, agreed to stay with Hannah, as he did not want to be at the church service. I was in a dilemma. I even phoned Pastor Jim Smyth to ask if it was possible to not bring the casket into the church for the sake of the children.

After consultation with Pastor Jim Smyth it was obvious that this could not happen. However, after a long conversation with Hannah we reached a compromise in which she would only come to the church after the casket had been carried out and then she would meet those who had come to sympathise with us. Samuel said he would do the same as Hannah, but Matthew felt he should attend the Funeral and Thanksgiving Service with me.

On the day of the funeral I cried in my bedroom before leaving for the church service. Just then the postman arrived with another fistful of sympathy cards and letters. I took time to open the first envelope and read the enclosed sympathy card. The reassuring words on that card were very timely and gave me a real sense of great strength and hope. They prepared me for Paul's funeral, for I knew that this was not the end. I lifted my heart in silent prayer to God and thanked Him for speaking to me through these words:

SAFELY HOME

I am home in heaven, dear ones,
Oh so happy and so bright!
There is perfect joy and beauty,
In this everlasting light
All the pain and grief is over,
Every restless tossing past,
I am now at peace forever,
Safely home in heaven at last.

Did you wonder I so calmly,
Trod the valley of the shade?
Oh! But Jesus love illumined
Every dark and fearful glade
And he came Himself to meet me,
In that way so hard to tread
And with Jesus arm to lean on,
Could I have one doubt or dread?

Then you must not grieve so sorely,
For I love you dearly still
Try to look beyond the shadows,
Pray to trust the fathers will
There is work still waiting for you,
So you must not idly stand
Do it now while life remaineth,
You shall rest in Jesus land.

When that work is all completed,
He will gently call you home
Oh, the rapture of that meeting,
Oh, the joy to see you come!

Another little bookmark I received in the mail that day had the following verse, which I held close to my heart on the way to the church:

Death hides, but it cannot divide,
Thou art but on Christ's other side,
Thou with Christ and Christ with me,
So together, still are we.

Chapter 2

Wiping Tears and Giving Thanks

My mind is still a blur trying to recollect what actually happened during the funeral and Thanksgiving Service at Limavady Baptist Church. I do know that the church was packed to capacity with many people standing outside. They had come from all over Northern Ireland. Many of Paul's colleagues from the medical fraternity were in attendance. Besides numerous Presbyterian ministers, pastors and Christian workers who had come to sympathise with Paul's mum, dad and us, people of the Hindu faith, Sikhs, Muslims, folk of other religions and none, joined the mourners at the church.

I can only remember people weeping as they embraced me and expressed their sympathy. Strangely, I did not weep. Visitors must have wondered how I could be so calm and strong, or maybe they concluded that I was a little removed from reality. On recollection, I think the latter was true.

Before we left our home Pastor Jim Smyth met with us and our immediate family to read the Scriptures for our comfort and to pray for God's help before we left for the church. Pastor Kenny Wilson, the recently inducted pastor at Limavady Baptist Church, conducted the service. Paul's friend and fellow surgeon, Robert Gilliland, was not in Northern Ireland on that day, and therefore, was not able to be present. However, in his absence, he sent a tribute to be read at the church, and in it he eloquently summed up Paul's life, his professionalism and his Christian faith.

Paul's best friend from his time at university, Dr Walter Boyd, gave an amusing but glowing tribute in which he recalled his respect for and friendship with Paul. I quote from Walter's tribute in other parts of this book, but he summed up his remarks as follows:

> Paul's illness was diagnosed in July 2002. We were saddened and stunned. Had God made a mistake? We all knew that, bar for a miracle from God, death was inevitable, but God's way was, and is still, perfect. Paul knew his time was short and had resolved that in whatever days he had left, he was going to use it for the glory of his Saviour and Lord. Only eternity will show what glory His servant, Paul Neilly, has brought to the Name of Jesus Christ.

These last two days have been strange in that while we prayed for Averil and the children, we did not pray for Paul. He does not need our prayers. Today he is absent from us, but present with his Lord. Today he is perfect; his disease has gone, and there is no more suffering.

Paul sought to glorify God while he lived. That was his chief desire. There is no doubt that he achieved that desire.

Rev Tom Shaw, our former minister at Ballycraigy Congregational Church, gave a most appropriate address, which was based on the words of the apostle Paul in 2 Timothy 4:6-8; "For I am now ready to be offered, and the time of my departure is at hand. I have fought a good fight, I have finished my course, I have kept the faith: Henceforth there is laid up for me a crown of righteousness, which the Lord, the righteous judge, shall give me at that day: and not to me only, but unto all them also that love his appearing."

Afterwards, Pastor Kenneth Wilson conducted the service and committal at the graveside in Limavady's local cemetery.

Although I cannot recall the details of the funeral proceedings, afterwards I learned from many people that the services had been conducted in an atmosphere of confident assurance and comforting thanksgiving, which was exactly as Paul would have wanted it to be.

Paul's parents and my family left Limavady after tea that evening, and by nine o'clock our house had emptied and everyone had returned to their own homes. It was obvious how heavy hearted they felt at leaving us, but at the same time they knew the children and I had to face the future as a family unit.

After the grandparents left I allowed the children to stay up for a short time. I think we all needed space to cry and try to come to terms with our new circumstances. A vital link had been broken; the head of our home had gone. Now it was important that we bonded together to help and support each other.

Just as I was about to send the children to bed at ten o'clock, the doorbell rang. It was Pastor Jim Smyth. He had come to pay us a late visit to read the scriptures and pray with us at the close of that difficult day. We did appreciate his thoughtful visit and support.

After the three children were tucked up in bed I remained downstairs for a very long time that night. I had no desire to go to our bedroom. I pondered on the thought that from now onwards I would always have to sleep alone in a king sized bed. When I eventually went to bed I rolled over to the side where Paul always slept. He was gone. Sadly, my arms were empty. I would never hug Paul again or be able to tell him how much I loved him.

The more I tried to sleep the more restless I became. Consequently, I got up and went downstairs to sit on the sofa where Paul had always sat beside me. I went back upstairs every hour and walked around the children's bedrooms. I wept as I watched them sleeping. My troubled thoughts were mingled with impulsive prayers to my heavenly Father: How are we ever going to get through this? How are the children going to cope growing up without a dad? What if I can't cope? What if I become ill and I also die?

When daylight broke on that next gloomy and grey morning, it was for me the first real day of my widowhood; my eyes were filled with tears, constant tears, which just would not stop. I was inconsolable. It was as if I had bottled up these tears during the three days since Paul had died, and now they could not be held back any longer. Hot salty tears streamed down my cheeks and dripped off my chin. My stricken mind continued to be tortured with what seemed to be insoluble questions: What am I going to do? How will I ever be able to cope?

The funeral was over, and this was only the beginning of a long journey in grief. I had been so naïve to think that I had already done some of my grieving during the previous seventeen months while Paul's health failed and faded. People often said to me that at least I had time to prepare myself for my husband's death. In many ways I did, but nothing could have prepared us for the grief that followed. The finality of death was extremely difficult to come to terms with. I did not know how to grieve myself, never mind helping my children to grieve.

Throughout the time that I had been at Paul's side and bravely watched him move through his deteriorating experience of cancer, I had loved and cared for him until his eventual death. I know that those months unconsciously played a role in preparing me for Paul's death, but in no way could they have prepared me for my aftermath of grief and distress.

Hannah, Matthew and Samuel were already downstairs, and I did not know how I was going to face them or how to talk to them. All I could do was weep. In my distressed state I remembered the words of Psalm 30:5: "Weeping may endure for a night, but joy cometh in the morning." I wished I could believe this to be true, but my tears still flowed, and I could see no light at the end of this dark tunnel

My lovely life, as I had known it, had ended three days earlier. The Lord had taken my husband home to heaven. My happy life with Paul and being constantly at his side was now over. I could hardly believe it or take it in. His death had left an aching void in my heart--an emptiness in our home, and our future looked bleak without him. I felt that anything from today onwards would just be a mere existence, a means to an end, and that end would be to try to be a mother to my grieving children. Nothing else really seemed to matter.

Even though I knew that Paul, a firm and faithful Christian, had gone to heaven, yet he had taken a large part of me with him. In marriage we were one flesh, and I felt as though I had been physically torn from him and he from me. I had learned that the word 'bereavement' has its root in a Germanic word meaning "to rob" or "to seize by violence". I felt as though I had been brutally mugged of my personal treasure and had been left with raw wounds which would not heal.

While I was overwhelmed with grief and sorrowed over my personal loss, my children needed me. I had to pull myself together and go downstairs to speak with them. Apart from exchanging, "Good morning, how are you?" a muted silence filled the air. There was a sense of supressed grief. But for me, even as I raked out the ashes and lit a fire in the living room, the tears still would not stop.

I spent the whole of that day with Hannah, Matthew and

Samuel. They seemed to act normally as if they were falling back into their usual routine of watching television or reading books. We had our meals, answered the telephone and read the numerous sympathy cards and letters of support.

In the early part of the afternoon I phoned Mark, Paul's brother who was the minister of Buckna Presbyterian Church. I think I must have wanted to reach out to speak with someone who had been close to Paul. Mark said that his wife, Hazel, had gone back to her work as classroom assistant and he was at home alone. When he asked how we were, I told him I had not stopped crying all that day. He confessed that he was feeling exactly the same and was constantly reduced to tears. On hearing this I decided to pack the three children into the car and travel over to the manse in Buckna, near Ballymena. We would be able to share our sorrow and weep with Mark.

The two of us talked over all the events of the previous week remembering Paul's final hours and the details of who had attended the funeral and what had been said. Mark reminisced to the children about their dad's boyhood and some family memories. Hazel arrived home in the late afternoon and kindly made our evening meal. Around the table we continued to console each other by sharing memories of Paul without our grief being too obvious to our children. Periodically Mark or Hazel would divert our conversation to more mundane matters, obviously trying to relieve us from being monopolized with our grief.

The time we spent with Mark certainly helped Hannah,

Matthew and Samuel, but for me, it only deepened my pain when I learned that Paul had asked Mark to keep a letter he had written and had asked him to give it to me only on the day after his funeral. Through streams of tears I read Paul's familiar handwriting by which he expressed his deep love for me and for our three children, how much we all had meant to him and his sincere thanks for caring for him through his months of illness.   It was heartbreaking for me to read the letter. I tried to imagine how it must have been even more distressing and heart-rending for Paul to write it. I read the short letter again and again and was so frustrated that I could not reply to Paul and tell him in return how much I loved him and how much our three children loved their daddy. I just wanted to cry out loud.

At the end of that day my eyes were still stinging from the rivers of tears I had wept throughout that first day.   I wanted to sleep, but sleep would not come easily. My mind was too active, and my heart was too sore. As I lay awake in bed, I thought about the vows we made to each other on our wedding day, fourteen years earlier, "till death us do part". I reflected on a piece that the soloist had sung at our wedding:

> *God hath not promised skies always blue,*
> *Flower-strewn pathways all our lives through;*
> *God hath not promised sun without rain,*
> *Joy without sorrow, peace without pain.*
>
> *But God hath promised strength for the day,*
> *Rest for the labor, light for the way,*
> *Grace for the trials, help from above,*
> *Unfailing sympathy, undying love.*

God hath not promised we shall not know
Toil and temptation, trouble and woe;
He hath not told us we shall not bear
Many a burden, many a care.

God hath not promised smooth roads and wide,
Swift, easy travel, needing no guide;
Never a mountain, rocky and steep,
Never a river, turbid and deep.

I wondered why she should have sung such a strange piece for my wedding day. The hymn speaks of God's faithfulness and strength in difficult days. Amazing that on what had been the happiest day of our lives that there should almost be forebodings of dark days to come.

My wandering thoughts helped me conclude that if I had known in 1989 that God was to give us such a short marriage, I still would have wanted to do it all over again. Even then, I still mulled over many questions, which had flooded my mind since immediately after Paul's death: What am I going to do without him? Why was this happening to us? How will I cope? What will become of the children? Why had I loved Paul so much? If I had loved him less, surely my grief would be less?

These recurring questions kept me awake to the small hours of the morning. However, the same questions helped me recall the first time Paul and I met.

Chapter 3

Reliving Our Dream

Although I had no answer to some of the unfathomable questions and the concerns that kept me awake that night, I had no doubts or regrets of why I had fallen in love with Paul and had loved him so much during our married lives. I remembered the first night we met. Ironically, I was already dating someone else at that time and never even imagined that this tall and handsome young doctor would play such an important part in my future. That first encounter happened one night when I was walking home along Belfast's Lisburn Road to Surrey Street after a late shift on Ava Ward 3 at the Belfast City Hospital. A car drew up alongside me, and the driver, Paul's good friend and medical colleague, Dr Walter Boyd, opened the window and called out to me, "Can we give you a lift home?"

I first met Walter, who was from County Tyrone, at the canteen in the Belfast City Hospital when my friend, Elma Hall, introduced me to him. Our paths had crossed several times after that, and because I knew him so well, I gladly accepted his kind offer and clambered into the rear seat of his car. It was then he introduced me to his friend,

Dr Paul Neilly, who was occupying the front passenger seat.

When we arrived at Surrey Street I invited them in for a cup of coffee and some supper. It was a little embarrassing when during their visit I had to excuse myself, leave the room and attend to a phone call from my boyfriend. Providentially, my relationship with that boy came to a sudden end a few weeks later, and on the rebound I determined that although I was already twenty-six years old, I would not be rushing into another romantic liaison.

I really did not think anything of that first meeting. In 1986, I was working as a staff midwife in Jubilee Maternity Hospital when the hospital authorities announced that those midwives who had most recently qualified would have to leave midwifery for a time and return to general nursing due to staffing problems. Although this was disappointing and unsettling for most of the other midwives I was confident that God had a purpose in it. I had already learned that when God closes one door it is because He is opening another--a better door.

Prior to qualifying as a midwife I had worked for eighteen months as a staff nurse in paediatrics. I was delighted when I discovered that in the administrative shake up I had been assigned to return to paediatric nursing.

Just at that time I met a nurse who was leaving the Belfast City Hospital to study for a Health Visitor Diploma at the University of Ulster in Jordanstown. The more I learned from this nurse about her course, the more I was persuaded that this would be my next career option. I loved working with children, and helping children would be quite a large part of a health visitor's programme. I therefore, applied to the Ulster University for admission to the Health Visitor Diploma course. I could hardly believe it when in that same week I received an offer of a midwifery post back at the Jubilee Hospital. However, I had already made the decision to go to university so I turned down the offer to return to the Jubilee. In the meantime I continued to work as a paediatric staff nurse at Ava Ward 3.

While I was looking after a little sick baby on Ava 3 I met Paul again. I had requested that a doctor come to the ward to take bloods for medical tests. In response to this request a young doctor arrived. It was Paul Neilly who was now a Senior House Officer at the hospital. At first, I did not recognise him, but then it dawned on me that it was him, now disguised by a freshly acquired beard.

Perhaps I was a little forward when I asked him, "Why have you grown that beard?" He said that he had come to the conclusion that having a beard was a time saving device whenever he was up all night and then had to rush to the hospital to do a ward round.

I think I must have agitated him a little by pestering him with a whole string of trivial questions while he was taking blood from the patient. My attention to Paul obviously distracted me from my work, for I failed to quickly cover the puncture site when he withdrew the needle from the child. As a result, some blood spilled onto Paul's zip-up cardigan. I did not like zip-up cardigans anyway and told him so. I probably should not have said that. The only way to redeem myself was to make him a cup of coffee and offer some biscuits. I already knew that Paul was a Christian. However, in the ensuing conversation over these refreshments I disclosed to Paul that I had come to the point of having a very low estimation of men since my last boyfriend had recently dumped me!

I honestly did not think I would see very much of Paul Neilly again after that second encounter. However, a few nights later Paul had reason to return to Ava 3 when I was on duty. Convinced in my mind that I was going to be a confirmed spinster I had decided to take up knitting as a sort of comfort hobby. The trouble was that I could not knit to save my life!

One night while I was on night duty on Ava 3 there was an unusual lull in our nursing duties in the small hours of the morning. I seized the opportunity and took out my knitting needles. I was happily knitting and following the pattern when suddenly I spied Paul Neilly walking up the steps and making his way into our ward. I panicked and desperately tried to hide my needles and wool before he could notice them, but I was not quick enough.

Although I was a little flustered and embarrassed at being seen with my spinster avowed knitting needles, I went to meet him thinking he had come to attend to the welfare of a patient. My embarrassment gave way to flattery when I learned that he had not come to the ward for any medical reasons or hospital duties; he had just come up to the ward at that unearthly hour of the night to visit with me.

Paul stayed for over an hour and during that time we quizzed and talked to each other about how we became Christians, our background and upbringing. I reminisced to him about my early life in the distant County Tyrone and, in turn, learned a lot about Paul and his childhood.

Chapter 4

Tyrone Among the Bushes

The small town of Castlederg in west Tyrone, with a population of less than three thousand, was a world away from anything that Paul knew, but that was my hometown. I was born in the town's small provincial hospital although my parents lived in the nearby village of Drumquin where dad was stationed. At that time he was serving in the famed B Specials, a branch of the Royal Ulster Constabulary (RUC). It was a dangerous career in those days as he and his colleagues had to patrol and police the vulnerable border region which was greatly exposed to terrorist activity.

After a few years dad changed his job from the RUC to become an area supervisor with the Northern Ireland Water Board. It was then that our family moved to Garvetagh, a small village community of less than a hundred people and several miles distance from Castlederg.

There were four children in our family: my older sister, Linda, my younger and only brother, Stephen and finally Elaine. Stephen is four years my junior, and Elaine is eleven years younger than I. I will never forget the day Elaine was born, for her arrival was on the same day that I started at the high school in Castlederg. Linda and I thought it was great to have a little baby in our home.

The primary school in the village was very small, but that is where I learned my reading, writing and 'rithmatic. I have many pleasant memories of the long summer holidays and spending a great deal of time playing the role of an imaginary homemaker. In our garden at the rear of the house, dad had made a playhouse for us and this contained everything we thought a house would need. I used to gather flowers from the garden, placing them in jam jars to be displayed on the table. I would then set the table and cook a meal for my imaginary husband coming home after a long day's work. There might even have been a tray of mud pies, dried in the sunshine earlier that day, and garnished with any available greenery. In my childish imagination this was a homemaker's dream, and I never got tired of my housework.

During those summer holidays I spent many long days with my cousin Lorraine Finlayson, who was two months older than I. We played endlessly at her home which was on the edge of a disused railway track and right beside a bridge over the River Mourne in Victoria Bridge. Lorraine had a much superior playhouse to mine, for hers had two rooms; mine was limited to one. Nevertheless, the two of us kept ourselves busy setting the table and cooking the meals for when both of our husbands would return home. Even at that young age I had an idea and tried to imagine what it would be like to fall in love and get married to the man of my dreams.

Lorraine's parents, Uncle Noel and Aunt Sadie, owned a caravan in Benone, County Londonderry. Prior to that it had occupied a site over the border in Rossnowlagh, County Donegal, but due to 'the troubles' in Northern Ireland at that time they felt it was no longer safe to travel back and forward across the border. Lorraine and I spent many summer days and evenings playing around the caravan until our hearts were content and our bodies worn out.

On one occasion I accompanied another uncle, Cecil Woods, who was making deliveries on his lemonade lorry. I was quite young, perhaps only four years old at that time. He later told me that I had been sitting up front with him in his vehicle and had begun to question him. "Uncle Cecil," I asked him, "do you like Davy?"

He started to name all the different Davys he knew. After each one I was apparently becoming more impatient, then in exasperation I said, "No, none of those 'Davys'. It's the Davy that you pour over your dinner."

He threw himself back in the seat and laughing his head off he said, "You mean "gravy". It's gravy and not Davy that you pour on your dinner Averil," he said.

I think I must have fallen silent after that infantile gaffe.

Of course, a girl's life then was not only playing house and pushing prams. The other pastimes in which we indulged included competing in games of marbles against the boys in our park. We not only acquired a degree of skill at playing marbles, we won a lot of the games and thereby gained more marbles. As a result, I had a huge sweetie jar full of large and small colourful marbles, most of which I had won from the boys. For me that jar was a treasure, and to keep it safe I hid it under our kitchen sink. I remember one day my mum gave me a smite of conscience when she asked me, "Averil, do you ever cheat?" I do not know whatever made her think of such a thing.

The nearby "Fairy Woods" on the edge of the village was our favourite place to hunt and wander during the long summer days. Why it was called the "Fairy Woods" I will never know for we never ever saw a fairy in that wooded area. The fact that the famous American frontiersman, Davy Crocket, had originated from the Castlederg area might have contributed to our venturesome spirit. On some days we would pack our picnic bag with juice and biscuits and head off on our bicycles. In those early days of our childhood we had no mobile phones or watches, so we returned home only when we felt hungry, and that was usually around dinnertime. Those truly were the happiest days of our lives.

While my dad worked in west Tyrone as an inspector for the Water Board of Northern Ireland, mum was always at home. I can recall her being in the kitchen with a snack ready for us to enjoy when we arrived home after school. I am very thankful for the carefree, happy and very secure upbringing we enjoyed.

Another area of my life for which I am thankful to God is that both mum and dad were converted at a tent mission in Castlederg in 1970. The Rev Ken Elliott of Bethany Free

Presbyterian Church in Portadown, had been the evangelist on that occasion.

Subsequent to that tent mission, our family started to attend the local Castlederg Free Presbyterian Church. While there I heard the plain message of the Gospel how that Jesus Christ gave His life for us at Calvary so that we might be forgiven and set free from the guilt of our sins. We were taught that Jesus Christ had taken the punishment that I deserved and in exchange He imputed to me His righteousness. I also learned that I was a sinner. Not only had I sinned against God, but I had been born a sinner. The Bible says, "For all have sinned and come short of the glory of God."

After hearing so much gospel preaching at church and seeing the change in our home since mum and dad had been converted, I knew that I needed to be saved. Their conversion did nothing to save me or my brother and sisters. I needed to make an individual decision to receive Jesus Christ as my personal Saviour. I thank God I took that step on Sunday, 8th December 1974, when I was thirteen years old. The Rev John Hanna, who has been a missionary with the Free Presbyterian Church in Spain for many years, preached about heaven on that Sunday morning.

When the congregation was singing the closing hymn I knew that if I were to die that very night, or if Jesus Christ should return before I had asked Him into my life, then my sinfulness and unbelief would keep me out of Heaven. Consequently, I would be forever separated from God and from my family for all eternity. I wept during the closing hymn. After the service had finished and others were filing out of the building, I remained behind to speak with the minister. After his counsel I was able to pray the sinner's prayer, repented of my sin and asked Jesus Christ to come into my heart and save me. That was a happy day. It would change and influence the rest of my life.

I remember that on the day after my conversion I was allowed to stay at home from school as mum was going into hospital for surgery. I brought the record player up to my bedroom and listened to Rev Ian Paisley preaching.

Now that I was a Christian, a child in God's family, I wanted to be out-and-out for Jesus Christ. I was keen to know how God wanted me to live for Him and what He wanted me to do with my life. A short while after my conversion I got the opportunity to teach a Sunday school class and start helping in the children's work in the church.

Now that we were into our teenage years, my cousin, Lorraine, and I also attended the Free Presbyterian youth camps on the Isle of Man, which were led by the Rev Cecil Menary. These were great times of spiritual blessing and great fun for us young people.

By this time I was studying at Castlederg High School, and as my time there was drawing to a close I had to start thinking and praying about a choice of my future career. After exploring various vocational possibilities, I felt constrained to apply for nursing training at the Belfast City Hospital in 1979. I was delighted when I learned that my application was successful and that I had been accepted to start my training in January 1980.

It was a big move for a teenage girl like me to leave the rural surroundings of west Tyrone and move to Belfast, the big city. However, the Lord answered prayer and I soon found the company of other Christian nurses who were also making the same transition from rural to urban life while doing their nursing training. I really enjoyed those three years of the general nursing course during which time I was able to stay at the nurse's home. While qualifying as a State Registered Nurse (SRN), I also forged lasting friendships with other Christian nurses such as Sandra Armstrong, who later became Dr Walter Boyd's wife, Jayne McDowell and Eileen Jackson. We all attended the Nurses Christian Fellowship each Monday night and were able to encourage each other and share times of fellowship at the hospital.

After gaining my SRN I signed up for midwifery training in May 1984 at the Jubilee Maternity Hospital, which was part of the Belfast City Hospital Trust. Because I had enrolled in the midwifery course I moved out of the nurses' accommodation at the hospital into rented accommodation, first in Kitchener Street and then in Surrey Street; both addresses were quite near to the hospital. Several of the nurses I had befriended became my housemates at these properties.

All through those years at the hospital I was greatly blessed to have parents who were praying for me every day. Looking back now I can see situations where I might have been tempted by the wrong company or have formed wrong relationships, but the Lord preserved me through it all.

I did not know that God was guiding me even when I was not conscious of His guidance. The Scriptures tell us that God holds the reins of our lives and guides us in the night seasons. That was exactly how it was with me.

Of course, that providential guidance had brought me into contact with Walter Boyd and Paul Neilly. It was Walter who introduced me to Paul, and I have no doubt that Walter had provided Paul with some of this information about my background.

Chapter 5

A Son of the Manse

Paul Neilly's upbringing was totally different from mine. He was a son of the manse, and, although born in the Mid-Ulster Hospital in Magherafelt, he was very much a refined townie; most of his childhood and youth were spent in Lisburn and Belfast, whereas I came from a rural town more than seventy miles away from the capital city. Paul had two brothers and no sisters while I had two sisters and one brother. Furthermore, and perhaps more formidable, he was a Presbyterian, and I was a Free Presbyterian. I suppose in many ways we were the most unlikely pair who would ever meet up and eventually tie the knot; however, God moves in mysterious ways.

Paul was the middle son of the Rev Jim and Mrs Florence Neilly, Stephen was his older brother and Mark his younger. The Rev Neilly and family had moved house several times in accordance with the ministries to which the Lord had called him. They served for five years in Tobermore Presbyterian Church before moving to Lisburn where the Rev Neilly served God for nine years at Sloan Street Presbyterian Church. The Rev and Mrs Neilly finally moved to Immanuel Presbyterian Church, formerly

Bethany Presbyterian Church, in Agnes Street, Belfast, where they remained for the next twenty-two years until their retirement from active church ministry.

Writing of his childhood Paul offered this:

> My parents not only loved God, they also served Him. My father had answered the call of God to be a Presbyterian minister, and my mother had been persuaded, perhaps against her better judgement, not only to marry him, but to also take on the responsibilities of a clergyman's wife.
>
> The three children that followed, Stephen, Paul and Mark, were affectionately known as salt, pepper and mustard. In my defence I maintain that I was not very peppery, but my younger brother certainly lived up to his name.
>
> As a result of my family background I was steeped in the importance of not only knowing that there was a God, but also that each one of us needed to have a personal relationship with Him before we could expect to get to heaven.

Even though Paul was raised as a son of the manse and his father was a noted evangelical Presbyterian minister, that did not make Paul a Christian. It takes more than that. Paul knew that he needed an individual relationship with Jesus Christ. Therefore, as a seven-year-old lad he trusted the Lord Jesus Christ as Saviour. Paul later wrote of that conversion:

I could not have realised how important that decision would be to ask Jesus Christ to be my own and personal Saviour. Even at that young age I felt convicted of being a sinner and was convinced that I needed to ask for forgiveness of my sins. It was on a Sunday afternoon during a Crusaders class in Lisburn that I was persuaded to ask Jesus into my heart. I walked home after the meeting with my older brother, Stephen, and knelt down with my mother in our drawing room and prayed the sinner's prayer.

I am grateful to both my parents for my Christian upbringing and the godly example they set. But, to be honest, I never really enjoyed being a son of the manse. I would have preferred some degree of anonymity in church life, but this was not to be. As the minister's son I tended to put on a good show, but underneath I had periods when only God knew how rebellious I was towards Him. Thankfully God remained faithful to me.

My father was not only a minister, but he also had important links with the Lord's Day Observance Society, subsequently becoming its chairman. As a result, I had quite a strict Christian upbringing and, at that time, was quite resentful. However, I now appreciate the discipline I experienced and feel that it is a lack of discipline that is destroying both the church, as we know it and society in general.

Paul's school life began with P1 at Brownlee Primary, Lisburn where his mother was a teacher. For the rest of his primary school education he was moved to Harmony Hill Primary School, which was also in Lisburn. From there he gained entrance to Belfast Royal Academy when his parents moved to Belfast and lived nearby on the Antrim Road. Although Paul spoke with a little distain of his boyhood days at school, yet he had his sights firmly fixed on accomplishing definite goals on which he had set his heart early in life. He believed that God had a plan for him, just as He has for every Christian. Paul wrote of those early ambitions:

> I saw school and education as an interruption to what could otherwise have been an enjoyable life. With my parents insistence that nothing in life comes easy I worked just hard enough to pass my examinations. It was not until I reached sixth form that I realised if I wanted to be the doctor in the family, which I believed was my calling, that I had better knuckle down to study. Recognition of the importance of hard work in reaching this objective nearly came too late. As a result I had to spend an extra year re-sitting two 'A' levels at Belfast Technical College to achieve my goal.

Paul's mother also shared a few thoughts about Paul's early childhood. Of course, as a mother she thought the world of all her sons and remembered her middle boy, Paul, as a very good baby and an adorable little lad.

I have only good memories of Paul. When he was only a little boy in Lisburn he brought the family presents from a day trip to nearby Dunmurry. He always was quite inventive and creative, and this got him into trouble when he built a place where he was able to sit up a tree in our garden at Clonevin Park in Lisburn. Some neighbours complained that our Paul was spying on them from his perch up the tree.

On another occasion he kept a dead frog in a box until it had shed its flesh and dried up as he wanted to know what a frog skeleton looked like. Perhaps this was a precursor to the medical career he would pursue in years to come.

Although the Neilly boys were reared in a manse, life in that home did not lack for boyish mischievousness, cunning pranks and lots of fun. Paul's brother, the Rev Mark Neilly of Buckna Presbyterian Church, gives some insights into life with the Neilly boys in the Presbyterian manse:

My brother Stephen and I have very fond memories of Paul. He loved to have fun, and as brothers we did all the usual things together, even though Paul was seven years my senior. I soon discovered that older brothers are built for the purpose of torturing their younger siblings, and that was something Paul did with great relish. At times he would sit on my chest, pin my arms to the ground with the use of his knees and flick my nose or rub muck over my face. Admittedly, this sort of torture usually came about because of something I had done to him.

Another preferred form of brotherly cruelty was to lay me upside down on the stairs, at which point Paul would start to throw things down at me from the upstairs landing. He knew my only means of escape was to slide down the stairs on my back, generally only coming to a stop when my head hit the wooden panel at the bottom of the stairs. We had the usual fights where we would each try to inflict the maximum amount of pain on each other--although it must be said these were all in good spirits. I don't think we ever had a fight in earnest.

Ever since I was a little boy I always wanted to be like Paul. One of the ways in which I tried to emulate him was in the area of swimming. Paul was a fantastic swimmer and actually got a Major Colour's (burgundy) blazer in Belfast Royal Academy to mark his swimming achievements. Paul and I were never in the Academy together, but during the school holidays he would take me to the open swimming sessions and teach me how to swim competitively. As a result, when I eventually did get into Belfast Royal Academy, I also went to the early morning swimming sessions on Monday, Wednesday and Friday mornings, along with the Life Saving classes on Tuesday and Thursday afternoons. Paul's swimming prowess was so well known in the school that I always felt I had a lot to live up to.

Sometimes Stephen and Paul were asked to look after me when mum and dad were going out. On one of those occasions Paul decided to take me for a ride on his bicycle. I was probably six or seven years old at the time, which meant that Paul was in his early teens. He placed me on the seat of the bike as he began pedaling to cross the four lanes of traffic outside the manse on the Antrim Road. Everything was going fine until I put my foot in the spokes of the wheel and everything ground to a halt--including the four lanes of traffic. The night I spent in the hospital was much preferable to the lecture Paul afterwards received from my shocked parents.

Paul was always very good natured and slow to anger. However, when he formed an opinion about a person, very little would ever change his mind. The three of us got on fairly well as brothers; however, there were times when we infuriated one another. On one occasion Stephen was reversing his car in the driveway as Paul was arriving home from university. When Stephen had started to reverse there had been nothing in the driveway behind him, so he was somewhat surprised and annoyed when he felt a jolt and heard a smash. He had reversed straight into Paul's car. A dispute started as to who was at fault. Each blamed the other until the dispute deteriorated into a heated argument. At that point dad's diplomatic abilities were required to restore the peace.

Of course, Paul was not slow on pulling pranks on Stephen and me. He used to loosen the bottom of the saltcellar so that when we picked it up the contents spilled over the table. Worse still, he sometimes placed an object on top of the door so that when we pushed it open we got a shock when that object fell on our heads.

Paul was always very kind-hearted and thoughtful. Every Sunday afternoon he visited elderly people linked with the congregation of Immanuel Presbyterian Church and took tapes of the services for them. Although he was only expected to drop the tapes at the various addresses, he took time to go in and visit with the elderly folk. These shut-ins really appreciated those weekly visits from a young man.

Paul was also very involved in the various organisations in Immanuel. He became a staff sergeant in the church's Boys Brigade Company and received the Queen's Badge for his adventures and work. For a year Paul was also vice president of the Christian Endeavour and served on the church's youth committee for several years.

At the same time I do not think Paul ever felt entirely at home in the Immanuel Presbyterian Church. He felt that life as a PK (a Preacher's Kid) was very difficult. For him it was like living in a fish bowl. When we did well in any of the church organisations we were told it was because our dad was the minister. When we failed to do well we were told that we should have been ashamed of ourselves considering our dad was the minister. We just could not win. At times Paul found this sort of warped thinking quite unbearable, and for that reason most of his friendships were mainly formulated away from the Immanuel Church. I had a somewhat better experience as a PK at Immanuel Church and always felt entirely at home there.

Chapter 6

Between Church and University

Although he was a studious young man, Paul had to work hard to attain the necessary grades in the "A level" examinations to gain entrance to the medical course at Queens University in Belfast. In fact, he was not successful at the first attempt; therefore, he had to re-sit the exams at the Belfast Technical College. That extra year of study in which he gained the necessary grades was a great investment for it would eventually open up a whole new future for Paul in the medical world.

The Immanuel Presbyterian Church and his father's Bible teaching ministry played a big part in Paul's Christian life and spiritual development during his teenage years. This growth was enhanced by a vibrant Christian ethos at Belfast Royal Academy and the fellowship with other Christian young people.

The step up to university in October 1981 brought all sorts of challenges to Paul. He not only embarked on a rigorous course of academic studies, but he was also exposed to all sorts of influences and temptations of varsity life on the university campus. Again he garnered support and encouragement of Christian friends like Walter Boyd, Lindsay Wilson, now a Free Presbyterian minister in Castlederg, Michael Nicholson who is a Consultant psychiatrist and Colin Patterson a GP in England. These friends helped Paul through those student years. All four of these medical students became firm friends and during the next six years and while at university, they supported each other until they qualified as medical doctors in 1986.

Dr Walter Boyd recalls those early days when he and Paul met and started as freshmen at Queens University, Belfast:

> To say Paul Neilly MD, FRCS, may sound to be quite a mouthful, but behind these few letters are years of study and dedication. I first met Paul in the summer of 1981 at a meeting organised by the Queens University Christian Union for medical students. Both of us had been accepted by QUB to train to be doctors; in October of that year I was assigned to be in the same study group as Paul. Some might call this fate, but I believe it was due to the providence of a sovereign God that we found ourselves in the same study or dissection group.

> I soon discovered that in our friendship it was a question of town meeting the country; Paul was the refined city lad; whereas, I was a not-so-cultured countryman. On the surface we had one thing in common: that was the

bond that binds all Christian believers together; both Paul and I had asked Jesus Christ to be our Saviour and Lord. Right from the first day, Paul's demeanour and life made it obvious to me that he was a Christian. I have no physical brothers, but in Paul Neilly I found a friend who would be closer than a brother.

From the first day we started at Queens we tried to learn a little about medicine; however, we also taught each other many other things. Because I was fresh up from the country Paul taught me that traffic lights in the city were in actual fact to be considered like a starter's gun. We, therefore, competed on the performance of his heavy green Mini against my yellow Sunbeam. As a result both of our vehicles regularly needed new parts to be fitted to them.

For my part, I taught Paul that milk did not come in bottles but was produced by four-legged animals known as cows.

I always found Paul to be both honest and modest. He rarely mentioned that he was the school's swimming champion. He loved Sunday and endeavored to keep it holy. On Sundays Paul usually visited the shut-ins from his dad's congregation or the elderly in the Geriatric Ward at Belfast's Royal Victoria Hospital.

Girls also featured in our lives during those

student days, but to be truthful, it was more talk than action. As students we needed to be dedicated to our studies. However, while on the subject of girls, I met Averil Young long before Paul and Averil ever became an item.

In the summer of 1984 I was on a medical elective in Africa, and when I came home I heard that a friend of mine had left a girl home from a social in Parkanaur, near Dungannon. He refused to tell me who that girl was. In the autumn of 1984 I was in Belfast City Hospital canteen when another friend, Elma Hall, came in with a nursing colleague Elma introduced me to that nurse as the girl whom my friend had left home that night from Parknaur. It was Averil Young.

On another night a medical student and I visited Averil and a few other nurses at their lodgings in Kitchener Street, which is not very far from the hospital. Subsequent to that visit, I met Averil at a band parade in Aughnacloy when two other girls, Ruth Campbell and Sandra Armstrong, accompanied her. Averil kindly introduced me to her two friends. The result of that meeting was that Sandra Armstrong later became my wife. Thank you Averil.

Paul also recalled those days at Queens while he was undergoing treatment years later:

At last I started medical school in 1981, and

there I met a lot of other people with the same aims in life. Most significantly, I met many who had a love for Christ, some of whom have remained dear friends. It was mainly the influence of good Christian friends that kept me on the straight and narrow in what was a rather hostile student world.

During my five years as a medical student I studied extremely hard, but looking back on it, I enjoyed every moment. My objective was not only to qualify as a doctor, which on its own was a daunting task, but also to become a surgeon.

Paul's friend, Dr Boyd, remembers other aspects of those student days:

Paul and I travelled the world. In the summer of 1984 Paul went on a medical elective to India. After we qualified we decided to go to Israel. When we landed in Tel Aviv, we had nowhere to stay. The two of us hired a car in which we not only travelled throughout Israel, but in which we also slept each night, totally oblivious of any danger. I still remember Paul's face the day I drove on the wrong side of the road in Jerusalem.

I went with Paul and Colin Patterson on a camping holiday to the south of England. I put a lid over my dad's old trailer and either Paul or Colin supplied the tent. By combining our efforts we managed to make a trailer-tent. On the first night of our expedition we pitched the tent on an open piece of land without realizing that a slope was not the best place for our camp. By daylight on the next morning all three of us had ended up in a heap at the bottom of the steep incline.

The Antrim Road manse was on the other side of Belfast from the university; that meant Paul did not have to be resident at the student accommodation. At the same time he had to be disciplined to continue his studies at home where his younger brother Mark was always on hand either to harass or enjoy the fun.

Mark writes:

Paul always loved animals, and since we were not allowed to have dogs or cats in our home while we lived in Belfast, Paul felt he needed to find some other sort of pet. He was very happy when he acquired a hamster, which he called, "Hammie". The little hamster had a routine every evening while Paul was studying in his room. It would climb up the right hand side of the curtains, walk along the pelmet and jump down onto a cushion, which Paul had strategically placed at the bottom of the left hand side of the curtains.

Hammie was a very happy little climber and jumper until one day when mum was tidying

Paul's room and removed the cushion. There he was, little Hammie, snugly nestled on the chair. Mother's frightening scream seemed to shake the whole house, and poor Hammie did not know what had hit him.

One day Hammie escaped from his pen and managed to fall down behind the kitchen units. Unfortunately, the little beast was not content to stay on the lower ledge behind the sink. Instead, it walked along to the high bit behind the oven, far beyond our reach and in danger of being starved or roasted alive. Paul and dad had to make a little cradle and then lower it down on string behind the oven to pull poor wee Hammie back up to safety again.

On another occasion Paul indulged in having some budgies take up residence in our home. For most of the time they flew freely around our living room and seldom were confined to their cage. That worked well except when they would occasionally sit on the back of a seat and deposit their mess on the upholstery. Due to the design of the chair the unsuspecting victim would not realise the dirty deed the budgie had left behind until he or she put their hand on the seat. That unpleasant discovery brought some loud threats of what they would do to Paul or to his feathered friends. Paul also kept a variety of tropical fish in two large tanks in the entrance hall of the manse, but, thankfully, they did not give us too much trouble.

Paul enjoyed the outdoor life and took an interest in gardening. He started off with a sizeable vegetable patch in the back garden at the manse. Eventually, he and dad constructed a glass house to enable the growth of tomatoes. However, when they were erecting it Paul managed to slice his finger on a pane of glass. While Paul, who was studying medicine, was able to handle everyone else's blood, he could not bear to see his own and instantly felt faint when he saw the blood flow from his finger that day.

One of our shared interests was cars, especially the fast and sporty brands. Every year we went to the Motor Show at the King's Hall in Belfast. We made it our objective to try to sit in as many new cars as possible. Paul was a safe, but a very fast driver. However, I remember one evening when we were returning home from a church meeting in mum's little sea-green Renault 5. Unfortunately, the car did not arrive home that night in the same condition as when we had left the manse. It was a wet autumn evening, and Paul was going flat out with his boot to the board. Just then a car slowly pulled out from the roadside at a snail's pace into the path of our speeding car. Paul jammed on the brakes, which made mum's Renault 5 go into a skid and slide. Despite all of Paul's best efforts to control the vehicle he left a Renault-5-shaped indentation on the side of the elderly gentleman's car.

Paul's first car was a pea-green Mini, which he fixed up to make it appear more sporty. When he and dad re-sprayed the car from its bare metal, I could never understand why they did not change that rather disgusting shade of green for something a little more attractive. Paul added Cibie Spot Lights to the front of the Mini and a dual-tone air horn that was so loud it could have wakened the dead. When Paul turned on his spotlights they almost sapped all of the power from the battery.

On Wednesday evenings mum, dad and Paul always headed out to the midweek meeting in church, leaving me at home to complete my homework. I knew I had a two-hour span in which to finish my work and still have enough time to have some fun driving the cars up and down our driveway.

One Wednesday evening I decided that Paul's Mini would benefit from a bit of maneuvering by a self-appointed and particularly gifted driver. Paul always parked his car tight to the wall at the side of the front steps and below the drawing room window. On that evening, after driving back and forward as fast as I could, I took the Mini a little too close to the wall and managed to ram it into an iron rod which was protruding from the wall. When I got out to examine the damage I found that the rod had gone right through the back panel of the car and into the rear wheel.

When I made my confession of this misdemeanor later that evening I received my just punishment. Needless to say, the keys for the cars were never left behind in the house again.

Paul's next car was a red Mark 1 Ford XR2, a real sporty vehicle. Sometimes when returning home from church on Sundays, Paul would drive his car over the undulating Hightown Road. He wanted to see for how long he could keep the car airborne when he drove it at speed over a series of consecutive ramps which were designed to limit the speed of the traffic. Paul would put his boot to the board, and the gathering speed made the vehicle project off the third ramp and into the air for a considerable distance and then come down with a bang if not a crash.

After raking the life out of that XR2 Paul bought a Toyota Corolla GTi16. Every year the two of us would follow the Circuit of Ireland Rally and stand together for hours in wet ditches just to catch a glimpse of the rally cars scream past at horrendous speeds. Between the stages we indulged in our own bit of rallying with me acting as the co-driver and navigator, trying to read the map. On one occasion we were barreling down this tiny country road, only to discover it was actually a farmer's lane. When Paul realized he was travelling at speed towards the end of this country lane he slammed on the brakes and pulled the handbrake to avoid hitting the puzzled farmer. Understandably, we got some rather interesting looks from the frightened and irate farmer.

When Paul was going through his medical training at Queen's University he decided to practice his skills of taking blood from his younger brother. As a result my arm eventually resembled a pincushion. After some time of being Paul's guinea pig, I felt I had observed enough to be able to have a go at taking Paul's blood. After my first attempt the shutters were pulled down and that was the last time he allowed me to try to take his blood. It was also the last time I played the part of being his guinea pig.

I remember on one occasion an ingrown toenail was causing me severe pain. Paul and dad decided they would operate on it to sort out the problem. Paul applied the local anaesthetic to my big toe, but unfortunately he did not give enough to do the job properly. Nevertheless, it did not stop the two self-appointed surgeons hacking at my toenail. I am glad to say that since then I have never had any more problems with ingrown toenails, at least none that I was prepared to tell them of.

As the date of Paul's graduation approached he still had a clear ambition to reach beyond qualifying as a doctor. He still wanted to be a surgeon. He later wrote of this:

> I vividly remember attending a meeting for those in my academic year who were interested in becoming surgeons. The professor who addressed the gathering made it very clear that of the twenty-five or so in the room that evening, approximately only two of them would be successful in becoming consultant general surgeons, although also a few could become specialist surgeons.
>
> When I heard this statistic I reckoned that the odds were stacked against me. However, ten years later, as a junior doctor, I was one of three doctors in my year to become a general surgeon. I was finally appointed as a Consultant General Surgeon with an interest in Colorectal Surgery to Altnagelvin Hospital on 1st February 2000.

This is running a little ahead of my story, so let me get back to telling you how our initial friendship developed into romance and marriage.

Chapter 7

The Blending

That middle-of-the-night visit from Paul on Ava 3 when we spent more than an hour getting to know each other was only the beginning of a long road ahead. Over the next few weeks Paul kept "accidently" meeting me at the hospital when I was coming off duty or was about to start work. In those days he drove a little red Ford Escort MR2. Of course, I was not only delighted to have a ride in his sporty Ford, but it did not escape my notice how he always seemed to have some romantic music playing when I got in. The vibes were clear and strong.

Because we were Christians Paul and I had a lot of common interests and many mutual friends. Over the next five months Paul and I became firm friends even though we were not really romantically involved at that stage.

We also continued to have a close friendship with Walter Boyd and Pauline Carson. Pauline was a nurse and one of my housemates in the rented house in Surrey Street. Even though there was no romance, the four of us frequently went out for meals and special evenings or social events. I will always remember when Paul, Walter and Pauline decided to visit our family's home in Castlederg for my birthday in May 1987. Mummy went to a lot of trouble making a steak dinner for she knew that Walter enjoyed good food. The dining room, with its antique table and chairs, furnished with mum's best china, was on full display. Mum had done an outstanding job and it all looked so beautiful.

The birthday meal got off to a hilarious start when Walter went to sit down at the table. Mother's good antique chair suddenly collapsed under him and left poor Walter on the floor squirming with embarrassment. Initially, there was a stunned silence, but when we saw Walter lying in a heap and surrounded by splinters of wood, we all burst out laughing. I do not know who was more embarrassed, Walter or my mother. I do know that the ice was well and truly broken, and thereafter we had an unforgettable evening.

Several months later, on the night of 17th August 1987, Walter, Pauline, Paul and I had planned to go out together as we had done on many previous occasions. During that week my parents had come up from Castlederg to help decorate our rented house in Surrey Street. Paul brought over a ladder so that dad would be able to reach the high points in the hallway. We left dad to get on with the work while we joined Walter and Pauline for that evening as had been arranged.

When I returned home later that night, my discerning mum made a comment about how Paul and I seemed to get along so well. She commented to me that she thought we would make a lovely couple. I was a little flattered, but not wanting to betray it, I tried to discount her comment and make light of her supposed intuition.

Poignantly, without mother's awareness, earlier on that same night, while I was sitting in the rear of Walter's car, I began to sense that Paul was becoming more than a friend and a possible relationship was beginning to blossom. I was a little nervous, but was also excited. However, in order to protect my own feelings, I decided to back off from developing any possible relationship. I knew that I had feelings for Paul, deep feelings, which made me realise that even if he never asked me out, I would never be the same again, I would never forget him. I felt that after meeting Paul and developing this inexplicable attraction to him, it would surely mean that going out with any other boy would only be second best.

Later that night in the privacy of my bedroom I prayed that if Paul were not the person of God's choosing for me that He, the Lord, would remove these irresistible feelings I had for him. I did not know that God would answer that prayer so quickly.

I was off work the next day and spent the early part of the day helping mum and dad tidy up after dad's painting the previous evening. After lunch I left my parents back to the Belfast bus station. As had been arranged, Paul called by our house later that same day to pick up the ladders he had loaned to dad. I was a little cautious of betraying my mixed up feelings to Paul, but over a cup of coffee we began to talk about the previous evening and how much we had enjoyed it.

We were not very long into the conversation when Paul became quite serious and began to tell me how he felt about me. I was stunned but ecstatic. When he had finished I confessed to him how that I had been trying to supress my feelings for him and how I had prayed that previous evening. I even told him of my mother's intuition. Both of us felt the Lord was in this matter. To crown it all, Paul invited me out for a meal on the following evening. In spite of my indecision on the previous night I had absolutely no hesitation in accepting this special date.

Speaking of that date, it was on the 18th August 1987 that Paul first shared his feelings with me. For obvious reasons, that day became a red-letter day for us and was remembered every year thereafter.

After he left I reflected on Paul's approach. I knew that he had undoubtedly been weighing up the pros and cons of making this move and wanted to be sure that he was doing the right thing and making the right choice.

Of course, during those five "friendship" months when we met up at hospital or elsewhere, I also had been pondering and evaluating the likelihood of us becoming an item. The more I thought and prayed about the possibility of any romantic relationship with Paul, the more I found I was falling in love with him, and I could not stop it. That is why I prayed that if Paul was not God's choice for me that He would take away the overwhelming feelings I had for him. At the same time, in my saner moments, I could see that he was the type of fellow I would want to be married to. On the other hand, I was convinced that I would never be good enough or sufficiently intelligent for Dr Paul Neilly; there was no way he would have any romantic thoughts for me.

How wrong I was. I discovered later that for the same length of time, Paul had been praying and thinking exactly as I had been. Like me also, he thought that when he would finally ask me out on a date there was no way I was going to accept. He was sure ours was only a plutonic friendship and that I would turn him down.

For me, visiting the Neilly manse for the first time filled me with a little apprehension, but I need not have worried. Mr & Mrs Neilly received me very warmly and made me feel completely at home. Of course, I did not know how many other girls Paul had brought to the house before I arrived. I do know that Paul's younger brother, Mark, went out of his way to make sure that the girls Stephen and Paul brought to the manse would have an unforgettable memory of life in the Neilly home.

Mark explains:

> There were several occasions when I was able to reap my revenge on my brothers for all the pranks they had inflicted on me, their poor little brother. I noticed that when Paul or Stephen brought their girlfriends to our house the custom always was to take them straight into the drawing room. However on one occasion, Paul made a fatal error and decided to prepare a tray full of sandwiches prior to picking up his most recent girlfriend. He was

so keen to create a good impression on her that he had used mum's best china, made and cut the sandwiches into dainty little triangles and then covered the whole tray with a linen cloth.

While he had gone to pick up his sweetheart I decided I would improve his pretty presentation. I placed a dirty bar of soap and a scrubbing brush on the tray to help the decoration. I also felt the sandwiches were a little bland so I replaced the grated cheese with grated soap. I replaced the sugar in the sugar bowl with plenty of salt to create a more interesting flavour in the tea.

When Paul arrived with his girlfriend he ushered her into the room while I sat at the top of the stairs waiting to hear their anticipated reaction. On reflection, I really should have chosen a rather more distant location to wait, for it did not take Paul too long to find me and inflict more pain on his mischievous little brother. As I recall, Paul did not call me by any endearing names like "little brother". He called me by other names and gave me such a spanking that certain parts of my body were sore for days afterwards. Nevertheless, I was immensely comforted and took great delight watching Paul checking his food for weeks afterwards in case I should have doctored it again.

I was also able to make a good impersonation of Paul and talk like him when answering the telephone. This allowed me to find out some interesting information by pretending to be him when some of his friends called.

It did not take very long for Paul and me to fall in love with each other. We seemed to gel right from the start. After three months, Paul told me that he loved me; I was able to say that I felt the same about him. However, the frequency of our times together had to be restricted and controlled because of the career commitments both of us were pursuing. Although Paul had already qualified as a doctor he always had an ambition to become a general surgeon and had a particular interest in colorectal surgery. To be able to realise this ambition he needed to spend a lot of time in the study besides attending to his already heavy workload and tight schedule at the hospital.

During this same time I embarked on the Health Visitor Diploma course at the Ulster University, and that kept me very busy. Although this meant that we had very little free time, we were able to make time and enjoy outings together. There was no doubt that my change of career from nursing had come at the right time. The 9-to-5 weekday hours of the university course allowed us to see each other at the weekends, otherwise our time together would have been very limited.

Chapter 8

On the Way to the Altar

At the time Paul formally asked me to go out on a date he was on a very hectic schedule. Besides working long hours at the hospital, he had already started studying for his Fellowship of the Royal College of Surgeons' (FRCS) exams. Furthermore, I had already started the Health Visitors' Diploma course at Ulster University. Consequently, we managed to see each other only for short periods. Even then, Paul would always finish our time together with a little word of prayer, no matter how short his visit was. He often became discouraged during those long periods of study, and to get away from it all he would travel over to Surrey Street to visit with me for an hour before returning for another few hours with his books.

In December 1988, less than eighteen months since we went on our first date, Paul proposed to me one Sunday afternoon in Castlederg. We were sitting on a little two-seater sofa in our home when he popped the question. That special little sofa now occupies a special place in our Limavady home. Not only had I no hesitation in accepting his proposal of marriage, mum and dad both appeared to be happy with our news. Dad told Paul that he had been wondering for a long time when someone would take me off his hands.

Paul briefly summarised those few years of our courtship in his book "The Cutting Edge" while he was a patient undergoing treatment:

> Along the way I met the girl who was later to become my wife. She was a nurse, and a Christian friend, Walter Boyd, who was also a doctor, introduced us. He spotted her walking home from work and reckoned she deserved a lift home. I sometimes joke that this was the beginning of the end and that the downward spiral continued until we finally tied the knot in 1989. Of prime importance to me was that Averil was a Christian. She has taught me patience and the importance of taking one day at a time in our Christian walk with God.

The excitement had already begun. Our wedding date was set for the 19th August 1989, exactly two years to the very day since Paul had asked me out.

When Paul arrived back home in Belfast that Sunday night after proposing to me, his mum was in the kitchen. He broke the news to her that he had just asked me to marry him. Mrs Neilly was taken aback and a little surprised. However, after Paul went to bed she sat down and wrote him the following little note that was waiting for him when he awoke next morning.

Paul,

You took me so much by surprise and left so quickly. Averil is a really nice girl and has been so good for you. In fact, I might say that if I had been choosing a girl for you, I couldn't have chosen any better, and that's saying something when it comes to what a mother would choose for her son! You are very well suited.

Love,

Mum.

On the following week, we went along to Lunns, the Belfast jewellers, and picked out a little three-diamond engagement ring; the three stones simply expressed those three romantic words, "I love you."

The nine months until our wedding were filled with all the usual enthusiastic, but at times frustrating preparations which most couples experience. I know that the time flew in quickly, and before we knew it the big day was upon us. Just a month before the wedding I qualified as a health visitor in July 1989.

Because Paul needed extra time off work for our honeymoon he had to be on the hospital ward right up until the evening before our big day. After speeding all the way from Belfast to Castlederg he arrived in time for the rehearsal at my church, which had been scheduled for later that night. After we had gone over all the details of the wedding with the minister, we emerged from the church only to be greeted by a waiting gang of friends who quickly kidnapped us and tied us up in an open trailer. The unruly, but friendly, mob then drove us around Castlederg several times with car horns blasting and loud shouts calling the attention of all and sundry to behold the spectacle of our predicament.

One of the ladies from our congregation was a cook, so she had turned up with a few containers of leftover food. This slop of flour and raw eggs was hurled at us until we were left in a fine mess. Paul had a mallen streak, a shock of white hair midst his otherwise dark hair, and this generally made him look quite distinguished. However, on that night both of us were completely drenched in white, sticky goo from head to foot. We needed to thoroughly scrub up before the next day, our wedding day, 19th August 1989. It had finally arrived.

On the morning of our wedding, I woke very early, jumped out of bed to pull back the curtains and look out of the window. To my dismay I discovered that it was raining. As a matter of fact, it never stopped raining throughout that day until late that evening. However, I was determined that the rain would not dampen my spirits or spoil our special day. I decided to go back to bed for another few hours. As I drifted back to sleep I was struck by this pleasant thought; by this time tomorrow, I will be starting my first day of marriage as Paul's wife. I could not wait.

The wedding took place at Castlederg Free Presbyterian Church. Our minister, Rev David Fletcher, and Paul's dad, Rev Jim Neilly, officiated at the service. Rev Stephen

Neilly, Paul's older brother, was best man while Dr Walter Boyd played the role of groom's man. My younger sister Elaine and a cousin, Julie Young, were my bridesmaids. It had been arranged that my older sister, Linda, would be Matron of Honour, but then she discovered that she was going to be a mum, so that ruled out her plans.

Paul's close friend, Dr Lindsay Wilson played the organ that day and Mrs Jean Beck from Immanuel Presbyterian Church was the soloist. I have always remembered the two pieces, "He Restoreth My Soul" and "God Hath Not Promised". It was this latter piece that would live with me again and replay in my mind all through the days of Paul's illness and my subsequent grief.

The joyous wedding reception was held at Thomas Doran House, Parkanaur, near Dungannon.

We did have a few hiccups during the day. We had chosen two vintage cars to take us from the church to Parkanaur, which is at least an hour's journey at a reasonable speed. On route to the reception Paul leaned forward and asked the driver if he would not mind going a little faster as all the wedding guests were flying past us in their cars. The courteous driver informed us that he had to limit the vintage vehicle to a certain speed due to its age. It was our first lesson in patience as newlyweds, and consequently, we arrived for the reception later than everyone else.

After the activities of the day and festivities of the reception we left the wedding party and rushed to the Belfast International Airport, more than forty miles away. We were alarmed to find that when we arrived at the designated gate the flight had already closed. After all the happiness of the day we had now missed our flight to London. Paul used all the diplomacy he could muster to explain to the ground crew that we were honeymooners and how disappointed we would be to get started on the wrong foot. They kindly relented and allowed us through to board the waiting plane.

Our frustrations had not finished. On our arrival in London we gave the taxi-driver the name of our hotel in Marble Arch. From Heathrow we travelled to the centre of London. The driver drove round various streets near Marble Arch, but could not find our hotel. By this time it was getting to be ridiculously late, but after the driver made radio contact with his headquarters he managed to locate the hotel at about eleven o'clock. We were greatly relieved to have finally arrived, although by now we were exhausted. I sat down at the door of the hotel with the cases while Paul went to the desk to check us in.

To our consternation we learned that there was no room for us at this hotel. Seemingly, the honeymoon suite had been double booked by mistake. After a flurry of telephone calls the duty manager was finally able to get us a room in another hotel nearby. That meant us getting back into a taxi and trying to locate this other hotel. We finally got to our room at almost midnight.

The next morning we learned the news of a terrible tragedy, which had happened in the early hours of that morning on the nearby River Thames. Although we were still full of marriage bliss and the glow of all the wedding celebrations of the previous day, we were brought down to earth when we heard that the luxury pleasure boat, The Marchioness, had sunk on the Thames after being run down by another river vessel, the Bowbelle dredger. Apparently they were having a private birthday party on board the Marchioness at the time of the collision. Fifty-one people had drowned and many others were seriously injured.

Later that day we attended the church services at the famed London Metropolitan Tabernacle, sometimes known as "Spurgeon's Tabernacle". Although we enjoyed the services we were conscious that the tragedy on the Thames had cast a pall of gloom over London that day.

Two days later we flew out to the Dominican Republic for our two-week honeymoon.

Chapter 9

Making Roots

We set up our first home at 21 Glenwell Park in Glengormley. A little plaque we had received as a wedding present occupied a prominent place in our home and expressed our prayer and aim as a family: "As for me and my house, we will serve the Lord." Accordingly, Paul set out a few 'ground rules' at the outset of our marriage, the first of which was that we would have a time of prayer and devotion together each day. The second ground rule was that we would never go to bed with any ill feeling still remaining between us.

Of course, I fully agreed with these in principle. However, one day during our honeymoon we had spent a full day touring on horseback. We arrived back at the hotel that night absolutely exhausted. I went to bed and fell fast asleep while Paul watched some television. He came into the bedroom to waken me at 10.30 p.m. so that we could have our daily Bible reading. I was not too happy to be wakened out of my deep sleep to have our daily devotional. Afterwards we laughed about it, for Paul's two ground rules had been broken in that one night and while we were still only on our honeymoon.

Soon after our arrival in Glengormley I was offered a
health visitor's post in the local health centre. With Paul's
long hours at work and study at home, I do believe my
career choice, with 9-5 weekday hours, was a great
blessing. Otherwise, our time together would have been
very limited. Paul continued with his long hours of study,
research, writing papers, doing exams and attending
surgical conferences. When he was abroad on seminars
Paul managed to contact me every day in spite of any time
differences.

Being married to Paul was everything I had expected it to
be. He gave me so much confidence in myself, and I felt
so secure in his love. His sincere devotion to the Lord also
challenged me to spend more time in Bible reading and
prayer. I think the love I had for Paul stemmed from the
respect I had for him and the love he had for His Saviour.

We tried to visualise our marriage union as a triangle with
Christ being at the apex, the uppermost point. The
husband and wife are represented on the base at the lower
two angles. With Christ as the head of our relationship
we felt that the closer Paul and I got to Christ, the closer
we would be drawn together. It very much was a
three-fold relationship.

Did we ever argue or have little tiffs? Of course we did,
but nothing that could not be sorted before the end of that
day. We always made it a point of talking to each other
every day, even if it was only for a couple of minutes by
telephone.

God blessed our home with three wonderful children;

Hannah was born in November 1991; Matthew followed in January 1993, and Samuel came into the world in December 1995. Our family was complete and our lives were full. I know that life in the Neilly home was both busy and challenging. Often I would tell our three children that their initials collectively read H. M. S.--His Majesty's Service. We prayed and longed that all three children would end up in the Lord's service.

Paul referred to those years we spent in Glengormley:

> After setting up home initially in Glengormley, we had three children, Hannah, Matthew and Samuel. At the time of my father's retirement from full-time ministry we started attending Ballycraigy Congregational Church. While there we were very blessed by the ministry of the Rev Tom Shaw whose pastoral care, in human terms, was second to none and continues to this day.

As Paul said, the Rev Tom Shaw was a great help to our family while we were living in Glengormley. Tom recalls the Neilly family's arrival at the Ballycraigy Congregational Church and the rapport he and his wife, Mabel, developed with them:

> At Ballycraigy Congregational Church we were delighted when Paul and Averil Neilly and their young family began attending our church in the mid 1990s. I knew that Paul's dad had recently retired from Christian ministry at

Immanuel Presbyterian Church in Belfast where Paul and his family had previously worshipped since their marriage in 1989. What even pleased us more was that the family did not come to Ballycraigy as casual visitors. They had arrived to make our church their spiritual home.

Right from the outset it was obvious that they were a committed family, committed to the church and to the Lord's work. They seldom ever missed the Sunday services although on occasions, Paul was on standby for a call from the hospital, and therefore, now and again, he had to leave a church service to attend to an emergency at the hospital.

They not only enjoyed the ministry of the Word of God, they also became involved in many departments of church life. Hannah, Matthew and Samuel were regular in their attendance at the Sunday School and midweek children's meetings. My wife, Mabel, when possible, was able to include the children in her various choirs for special occasions.

In spite of the demands on Paul's time and energies as a surgeon during the day, he still found time to be part of the church's outreach programme, either on door-to-door visitation or other evangelistic efforts. He not only participated in this outreach, but was also well equipped in handling the scriptures and reasoning with those who had differing views that were contrary to the Bible.

Paul was also very faithful in his attendance at the weekly church prayer meetings, and even early on Sunday mornings he would join with us to seek God's blessing on the ministry of the Word for that day. No doubt influenced by his dad's position as chairman of the Lord's Day Observance Society, Paul was also very concerned for the sanctity of the Lord's Day.

Perhaps Paul's devotion and sincerity impacted me most when he shared with me how he had gone off by himself to the Belfast Lough shore. He wanted to be alone with God and his Bible. He told me that he felt at that stage, due to his busy medical commitments, he had missed out somewhat in his walk and relationship with God. During those hours alone with His Lord he wept over what he felt was the coldness of his heart and how lukewarm he had become towards the things of God. Before returning home that evening he was able to put these matters right and rekindle again the flame of love and devotion to Jesus Christ and His service.

Paul and Averil also maintained a very keen missionary interest, and I well remember when they went off to Kenya for several weeks to relieve a missionary surgeon. That trip made a great impact on them and it seemed at that time that they were destined for more hands-on missionary involvement. However, the Lord had other plans.

Everybody at Ballycraigy was heart-broken when Paul and Averil announced that they were leaving Glengormley and moving north to set up home in Limavady. Of course, we were also very delighted to learn that this move was brought about because Paul had been successful in acquiring the position of consultant surgeon at Altnagelvin Hospital in Londonderry. I was aware that such a high position had been Paul's aim for sometime.

In 2001, just a few years after the Neilly family moved to Limavady, Mabel and I left Ballycraigy to accept a call to Donaghy Congregational Church, which is near Cookstown. During our time there we continued our close friendship and rapport with Paul and Averil. Periodically they came to visit us or attended our church services at Donaghy, and we were always glad to see them.

Our lives became even more challenging in January 1996, when we packed our belongings and left Glengormley for New Zealand. It was an ordeal to move to the other side of the world with three children, all of whom were under four years old; Samuel had only arrived into the world five weeks earlier. However, in the course of his pursuit to gain his FRCS, Paul had been offered a specialist year working alongside Mr Graham Hill, who was Professor of Surgery at The University of Auckland and a noted Christian surgeon who had been engaged in researching advances in colorectal pouch surgery. This was Paul's desired field of study.

During that year Paul gained much experience. He studied hard and worked very long hours at the university hospital. However, the hard work paid off when Paul was able to complete his M.D. (Doctor of Medicine) while there.

I found that year down under in New Zealand to be difficult at times. It was hard for us trying to adjust to living in a strange country with three small children. Furthermore, Paul was rarely at home with us, and his absence made me miss my family and friends all the more. Often when people enquired about our year in New Zealand Paul told them to ask me as I was the one who had lived there. He said that he just worked at the hospital.

At the same time, we did have special times together and have many happy memories of life in New Zealand. Paul's parents came to visit us for five weeks, and for two of those weeks we toured all over the beautiful South Island with them in a camper van.

We were also pleasantly surprised to discover that the pastor in a local evangelical church that we opted to attend was from Broughshane. During those twelve months, Pastor Colin Redmond and his wife, Lesley, became our dear friends. Catherine and David Van Dorp and their children also befriended us and helped me immensely with those all-too-frequent periods of homesickness. Another acquaintance, Fred Kane, who had immigrated from Castlederg forty years earlier, and his wife Deidre, became like surrogate grandparents to our children as did Jim and Val Beattie, also from Northern Ireland. God sent these dear friends into our lives and made them a great blessing to us.

While the year in New Zealand was a great benefit to Paul in the medical field, he later wrote of another observation, which very much reflected his own conservative and orthodox views:

> As part of my surgical training we spent one year in Auckland, New Zealand. There we saw the devastating results of charismatic renewal within the Church two decades previously. This resulted in a small contingent of evangelical churches with the remainder of the churches having been destroyed by liberalism, new-ageism and modern apostate movements such as the 'Toronto Blessing'. The church we attended was pastored by an ex-pat from Broughshane, Mr Colin Redmond, who has become a very dear friend. Unfortunately, since our departure from New Zealand in 1997 many of these small assemblies have been further damaged by internal disputes, which have again diluted the evangelical voice in a country with such a rich history of God's blessing.

> Despite the apparent evil influences on God's people in this country I was profoundly

affected by many of the Christians I met there. In particular, my trainer in Auckland Hospital, Professor Graham Hill, who was the first consultant I worked with who took time to pray with me and has provided on-going support during my recent illness.

Professor Graham Hill also passed away in Dunedin after a prolonged illness. His death notice appeared in the Dean's diary at the faculty of Medical and Health Sciences on 1st March 2013.

On the inside cover of his book, "Surgeon, Scientist", with the sub title, "Adventures in Surgical Research", which was written by Graham Hill, he wrote in my copy in May 2006, "To Averil, In these pages you will find a record of Paul's outstanding work during your time in New Zealand."

Our baby, Samuel, began to grow and soon developed lovely ginger locks. These always drew a lot of attention when we shopped at the local supermarket. We often laugh when we remember the day Gran and Papa Neilly arrived in New Zealand from Northern Ireland. Soon after they deposited their luggage in our home, despite the fact that they had just arrived after such a long flight, they decided to head out with us to the supermarket to do a large grocery shop.

Samuel proudly sat up on the front of the trolley, and the doting grandparents happily took turns with us to wheel Samuel and our purchases up and down the aisles of the shop. Somehow we got separated for a few minutes, but then we bumped into each other by chance at the cheese counter. After deciding on which cheese we should purchase, Paul and I went off by ourselves to do some more shopping in the store. Fifteen minutes later Gran and Papa met us again, but this time they were without the trolley, and there was no sign of Samuel. They were quite surprised at our reaction for they had thought we had the trolley with Samuel while we had been under the assumption that they were still pushing him around in the trolley. It was immediate panic stations. We frantically searched up and down the aisles of that supermarket for our lost son, never mind the purchases.

We were all greatly relieved when we eventually found him, totally unaware of our panic and still sitting contentedly at the cheese counter where we had left him, smiling at everyone walking past.

After Paul had completed his studies and the course which had taken us to New Zealand we left that lovely country in the height of the summer to return to cold and damp Northern Ireland in January 1997. Even though we had been gone for only a year, yet our children seemed to have become naturalised Maoris for they wondered why they could not run barefooted on Glengormley's streets during those dark January days.

The children quickly settled back into the British school system and I was glad to be able to return to work in Northern Ireland as a local health visitor. Meanwhile, Paul continued to study for Part 3 of his FRCS and finally qualified as a surgeon.

By late 1999, a post became available in Altnagelvin Hospital, Londonderry. Paul applied, was duly interviewed, and we were all delighted when he was accepted for the position. Paul had reached his goal and was finally appointed as a Consultant General Surgeon with an interest in Colorectal Surgery on 1st February 2000.

Chapter 10

Mountains and Valleys

With Paul's appointment to the new position at Altnagelvin we had to start house hunting in Londonderry. We eventually found a suitable property in Limavady and moved into our new home in July 2000, the same month in which Paul began his role as a consultant at the Altnagelvin Hospital.

In September the children were enrolled at the Central Primary School in Limavady, and I was able to resign from my health-visiting job and become a full-time stay-at-home mum.

Paul loved his new position as a consultant surgeon, although it brought many initial frustrations. We felt so blessed. Paul had accomplished his life's ambition; we were settled into our new home; the children had started at a new school; we had found a new church, and very soon we were making new friends. I recall Paul saying to me one day whilst we were out walking that he had all he ever wanted in life and that it could not get much better than this.

We often talked about our dreams and hopes for our future; we wanted our children to know the Lord Jesus as their personal Saviour and planned to help them work hard at school so that they could pursue their chosen careers.

Of course, we had our usual frustrations in raising our three lively and sometimes boisterous children. Paul and I were asked one day to go to the primary school to speak to Samuel's teacher. Apparently he had picked up a dying frog from off the path in the school playground. Soon the screaming girls scattered everywhere seeking a refuge while Samuel Neilly was having great fun in separating the slimy limbs from the poor frog and firing them at the terrified girls.

The first question the teacher asked his mum and dad was, "Have you not taught your children the value of God's creatures?"

As we walked back to the car, Paul, no doubt recalling the time when as a boy he also had kept a dried frog in his garden, took my hand and said, "That's my wee Sam. Like father like son."

Samuel seemed to be the one who was always in trouble. On another occasion, I was called in again to the school for a personal interview as Samuel had slipped down under his desk to tie his shoe lace to that of the girl who sat beside him. The unsuspecting girl subsequently fell to the floor when she tried to get up from her seat. I think Samuel was hurting more at the end of that day than the poor girl.

In 1999 we were able to travel to Kijabe, Kenya where, for two weeks, Paul was able to work at a mission hospital. We went to relieve Mr Andrew Hill, the son of Professor Graham Hill with whom Paul had worked in Auckland, New Zealand. Like his dad, Andrew also was a surgeon, and he with his wife, Lori, and their three children, worked with African Inland Mission. It was during our time in Auckland that I became friends with Lori, and it was great to be with her again in Africa.

This visit was a mountaintop experience for us. We all enjoyed it so much that Paul agreed to put our names forward for short-term mission work in order to give missionary surgeons in various countries a much needed break. Those plans did not work out, but God had other plans--plans which began with a gradual descent from our mountaintop experiences.

On the 14th December 2001, I went out to have a meal with other parents whose children attended the Central Primary School. We had a lovely time and arrived back home around midnight. As I got ready for bed I felt a little unwell, but did not dwell too much on it as I had eaten a meal quite late that evening. I awoke around 1.30 a.m. feeling very nauseated and experiencing an acute abdominal pain. I woke Paul to tell him I was unwell. He asked me what I had eaten. "Duck," I replied.

There was not too much sympathy in his voice when he answered, "What do you expect if you eat duck? Go back into bed; you most likely have food poisoning."

Two hours later I was up again being sick and in agony

with excruciating abdominal pain. Some duck, I thought. I woke Paul again to tell him I needed to get to the hospital as I was really unwell. He tried to persuade me to wait a little longer as he was reluctant to call the doctor out in the middle of the night.

The pain and nausea persisted, and by 5.00 a.m. Paul finally called Mr Bateson, another consultant surgeon, who lived close by our home. He kindly agreed to come over immediately. After examining me I overheard him telling Paul that there was a mass in my abdomen and that I needed to get to hospital as soon as possible. Paul was very upset. He quickly arranged for a neighbour to come over and stay with our children while he rushed me the eighteen miles to the Altnagelvin Hospital.

A scan quickly revealed that I had an ovarian cyst, which was close to rupturing. I was taken to theatre for immediate surgery. The fallopian tube, ovary and cyst were removed.

As I lay on my hospital bed recovering from the anaesthetic, my mind was in a whirl. This had all happened so suddenly. At the same time I was glad it was over so quickly, and now I would be able to recover. My children and Paul needed me at home.

My plans were changed a few nights later when the doctor came to tell me that they had detected early cancer cells in the ovary. Just to hear the word "cancer" frightened me. However, the doctor continued to say that he was confident that these cells had not spread elsewhere in my body. This sobering news really brought home to us that our lives were very much in God's hands and that we could not be certain about anything in this world.

By the end of February I was due to see the gynaecologist for a follow up examination after the surgery. During this visit it was suggested that I should go for further surgery and have a total hysterectomy to ensure there would be no recurrence of the malignancy on the other ovary. I had that surgery in March 2002 and thankfully, everything went well. Afterwards I was able to recuperate at home.

During my recuperation I had too much time to dwell on things, and many anxieties troubled me through those weeks. These fears made me realise just how dear my husband and children were to me. At the same time, when I was alone, I found myself thinking about the future for Paul and the children should I not get better. I became so anxious that I needed to know that God's presence was with me and He was in control of our lives.

In the middle of that month, March 2002, Paul needed to go to England for a surgical conference. Due to my recent surgery I was unable to drive our car so my mum invited us to go to Castlederg for those few days while Paul was away. She wanted me to be able to have the rest, which I needed. Furthermore, my father had recently been diagnosed with Lewy-body dementia, a form of dementia, which shares parallels with Parkinson's and Alzheimer's disease. For this reason, mum was needed at home and could not travel to us in Limavady.

Mum was also looking after Nathan, her grandson, each morning while his mother, Linda, was at work for a few hours. Nathan, who was nine years old, was only nine days younger than our middle child, Matthew. He and Matthew were great friends and playmates and nothing gave our boys more pleasure than a visit to Castlederg to spend play days with Nathan.

During those few days we spent with mum, it was obvious that Nathan was suffering with fatigue, lethargy, and excessive thirst. His dad and mum, Tommy and Linda, had already paid a visit to their doctor and all tests were clear. However, Nathan's symptoms continued to worsen.

Within a few days we returned to Limavady to be at home for Paul's arrival. A day or two later Linda phoned to tell me that Nathan had been admitted to the Erne Hospital in Enniskillen and that a scan of his brain revealed he had a brain tumour.

We were stunned, shocked for Nathan, devastated to think of what his mum and dad were going through. It just seemed impossible to believe that this was happening. Not only was this another sickness in our family, it also was much more serious than anything we had ever faced before.

I remember going into Paul's study to tell him the news. I asked if he would call a friend who was a neuro-surgeon as I wanted to be able to call Linda back with some reassurance or a measure of good news. Paul spoke to the surgeon, and he managed to find a bed for Nathan on the following day in Royal Belfast Hospital for Sick Children. However, there were no great words of hope that I could pass on to Linda. We learned that Nathan's condition would require surgery.

We were further devastated when we heard that the surgery in an attempt to remove the tumour, had not been successful. The surgeon said that the tumour was extremely hard and any further attempt to remove it could have put Nathan's young life at risk.

As a family, we felt helpless; all we could do was pray. Paul took me to visit Nathan, Linda and Tommy a few days later. Little Nathan was sitting up in his bed, talking to us all and seemingly, in good form. Alas, a few days later, his condition deteriorated and within three weeks of Nathan's first diagnosis, he passed into God's presence.

Our hearts were broken. We attended Nathan's funeral on the 2nd May 2002. His death had been so sudden and so unexpected. Our entire family circle was devastated. I wondered how we as a family were going to support each other and help Tommy and Linda through this great loss.

As I drove back to Limavady alone that night, I could not help thinking about Linda and Tommy and how they would be able to sleep that night after laying their little son, Nathan, in the newly dug grave.

Paul's parents had been looking after our children while we attended the funeral in Tyrone. After greeting them I quickly went around each bedroom to give our three children big and individual hugs. I wanted to hold them and make sure they were well after that difficult day. When I visited six-year-old Samuel's room he was still awake. He asked me if Nathan had gone to heaven. I reassured him that he had. Samuel further questioned me that if he had died would he also be in heaven as he had not as yet asked Jesus into his heart.

For a few moments I talked to Samuel about the importance of taking that step and suggested that he should give it some more thought before doing anything. After I said that I was ashamed of my action, but I was in a dilemma. I needed to get back downstairs to allow Paul's parents to leave for home as it was a long way from Limavady to Belfast. Fortunately, Samuel did not give in to my suggestion. He persisted, "But Mummy, I want to ask Jesus to save me tonight."

Feeling rebuked at my first answer I knelt down at his bedside and prayed with Samuel as he asked the Lord Jesus to come into his life.

Although I was sad I was so delighted at Samuel taking this vital step. I could not wait to phone Linda and Tommy and share the good news with them. I wanted them to know that Nathan's death had not been in vain.

We all felt that life would never be the same for our family again. We were out of our depth in knowing what to do for Linda and Tommy in the weeks ahead. Linda shared with me one day that she was finding it difficult to have the assurance that Nathan was definitely in heaven. She had been told over and over again that he was only a child, and therefore, there was no doubt that he had gone to be with Christ. Even then, Linda was troubled when she thought about all the children's missions Nathan had attended and wondered if he had heard God speak to him and maybe had rejected the offer of salvation.

This awful fear was unrelenting and prevented Linda from moving on through the grieving process. We earnestly prayed that God would intervene and help her. He did in a most remarkable way. A little boy who had been in Nathan's class at school told Linda that she should not be worrying as Nathan had witnessed to him about being saved. Even with this good news Linda still did not have peace.

A couple of weeks later, Nathan's teacher phoned to ask if she could visit Linda and bring Nathan's school books with her. That night, after the teacher left, Tommy and Linda picked up Nathan's class notebook, which was on top of the pile. They had never seen this book before, as the pupils did not take their notebook home. As they read Nathan's hand writing a deep sense of peace filled their hearts. At the beginning of the term, Nathan had to write a few lines about why he was special. He had given his reply in his class notebook and finished the paragraph of by saying, "I am special because I am saved!"

Peace flooded their hearts, that was exactly the reassurance Nathan's parents needed and had been longing for. God makes no mistakes, and His timing is always perfect.

Averil.

Paul.

Averil P.3.

Paul P.4.

Averil - Staff Nurse.

Paul graduates.

Walter, Paul & Colin. Aspiring 'Harley Street Doctors.' Summer 1987.

The Friendship 1987. Walter, Averil, Paul and Pauline at 'The Manse' 680 Antrim Road.

More than friends - engaged.

Averil's graduation University of Ulster, Jordanstown - Diploma in Health Visiting with Paul, Mum & Dad. 2 July 1990.

Paul's graduation. Paul, Lindsay, Andrew and Walter at Q.U.B.

Engagement 1988.

Signing the register.

Happy couple with parents.

The look of love.

Cutting the cake.

Paul's Mum and Dad.

Averil's Mum and Dad.

Averil's family.

Paul's family at Q.U.B. Paul's dad receiving M. Phil 1996. (Missing Paul & Averil - New Zealand).

Honeymoon in Dominican Republic. August 1989.

Our first anniversary. (Roses and grape juice).

F.R.C.S. Edinburgh. 1990.

The F.R.C.S. Fellow's Dinner Edinburgh.

Q.U.B. M.D. 1997.

M.D. Queen's University.

Hannah, 15 November 1991.

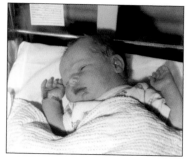

Now there are two. Matthew 10 Jan 1993.   Now there are three. Samuel. 15 Dec 1995.

Our home in Auckland, New Zealand 1996.

Neilly Family 2000.

Paul, Stephen and Mark, a few days before Paul's surgery, July 2002.

Paul and Averil prior to Paul's surgery July 2002.

Hannah.

Matthew.

Samuel.

Matthew and his cousin Nathan.

Hannah, Samuel and Matthew - New Zealand 1996.

Averil, Samuel, Matthew and Hannah - 2008.

Samuel, Hannah, Averil and Matthew - 2013.

Chapter 11

A Deep Trough

That summer of 2002 brought more challenges. Paul's health began to cause us considerable concern. For some time now he had been suffering from Irritable Bowel syndrome (IBS). Paul was always set in his mind, and no amount of hints on my part would get him to seek advice. He used to reply with "How can I get checked out in my own department, by my own nurses and doctors with whom I work every day?"

I could understand his predicament with this type of complaint.

At the beginning of July we went to the Lake District for a week's holiday. Usually during our vacations, Paul's symptoms would settle down, but on this occasion they did not. Furthermore, he did not want to be very much involved with the children's usual physical activities, which he would have normally done while on family holidays.

By the third week of July Paul had returned to work. One morning during that week he left home earlier than usual.

While I was still in bed he leaned over to kiss me goodbye and told me that he had something he needed to see to before he started work. He also said that he did not have time to read and pray, but that I should do it on my own. I quickly went back to sleep.

I overslept. When I awoke it was already after 9.00 a.m. Hannah, Matthew and Samuel were already up, dressed and heading out to play at a neighbour's house. I started tidying the house, and as I did Paul came to mind. I so wished he would get his health checked out as that would be one less worry. It was then I realised that I had not yet prayed that morning. I needed to take my burden to the Lord.

After reading and praying, I returned downstairs around 10.00 a.m. to make a cup of coffee. The telephone rang. It was one of the nurses from the Day Procedure Unit (DPU) at Altnagelvin Hospital. She told me that Paul had bravely endured a colonoscopy and that he needed me to go to the hospital and bring him home as he was feeling very uncomfortable.

It was the nurse's next statement that caused alarm within me. She asked if I had the children at home with me. When I answered in the affirmative, she asked if I could go to the hospital without them. That caused even more alarm, and I knew that something was not right.

My friend and neighbour, Jane, agreed to have the children stay with her while I was away in Londonderry. All during that eighteen-mile drive to the hospital I talked to myself and prayed that God would help me with whatever I might hear or meet on arrival at Altnagelvin. I knew that something was not right, and this was causing me an overbearing feeling of dread and fear.

I rushed into DPU and was quickly shown to a little room where Paul was waiting for me with Mr Robert Gilliland, a fellow surgeon. I do recall that the nurses did not make eye contact with me and gave evasive answers when I anxiously enquired how Paul was. It was only later I realised that those nurses and the other personnel present worked with Paul on a daily basis and were aware of the awful news I was about to receive. All of them were devastated.

Robert Gilliland hugged me and then left Paul and me alone. I searched Paul's face for an explanation of what was happening. He started to cry, "Averil, I am so sorry. I have had a colonoscopy and a CT scan and this has shown that I have a large tumour in my bowel. The scan also showed that the malignancy has already spread to my lungs. I was able to make my own diagnosis, and it's not good. I think, at the very most, I have ten months left to live."

I too began to cry. I hugged Paul and told him over and over again that it would be ok and that it was not his fault. "We will get through this. God will be there to help us," I tried to assure him.

The drive home is a blur. I cannot recall anything that happened from the time Paul told me of his diagnosis until we were back in our living room. At home we talked a little about the possibility of him having surgery on the

Friday when Paul would be a patient on his own operation list.

All sorts of questions were swimming around my mind: What are we to do next? What about the children? What about our parents, especially my mum and dad who were still grieving for little Nathan? I remember praying, "Lord, how much more can our family take?"

That night we told Hannah, Matthew and Samuel that dad had some cancer cells in his body and that he would be having an operation on Friday to help remove them. Paul was very concerned for Hannah because she was starting to work for her 11+ exam, and he did not want her to be unduly alarmed at this stage.

Later that same night Paul's two closest friends, Walter Boyd and Lindsay Wilson, came to visit us along with Rev Tom Shaw, our previous minister at Ballycraigy Congregational Church. God really ministered to us that night through their conversation and prayers. Before the evening was over we were able to hand the whole situation over to the Lord and go to sleep.

Paul later reflected on the trials our family passed through in 2002:

> Just over a year ago I had an article published in the Life Times magazine. Unknowingly, I was describing a medical condition that was to change my own life and perhaps also accelerate my promotion to a better place. None of us know what the future holds, and if we did, perhaps we would not be so complacent about

life, death and eternity.

Until this point in my life my daily schedule had been very busy, and I, like others, had my fair share of frustrations. However, I was satisfied that I had arrived at where I wanted to be in life and had achieved most of my goals. I had a loving wife, three young children with a bright future, a career with many rewards and most precious of all, I had the assurance of eternal life. Over recent months it has been my relationship with God that has been the pivot around which my life has rotated.

As a medical student and a junior doctor, having cared for patients with terminal illness, it became my firm desire never to have cancer myself and to only die a peaceful death in my old age. This hope extended to my wife and family, but since the winter of 2001 we discovered that God had different plans. We were to experience problems that would turn our lives upside down.

On 14th December 2001, after returning from a pre-Christmas meal with friends, my wife developed excruciating abdominal pain and within twelve hours was on an operating table in Altnagelvin Hospital. She had a malignant ovary and although the disease appeared to be at an early stage, the certainty of our mortality was made that bit more real. She then required a further operation in March 2002 to try and prevent a recurrence.

If this weren't bad enough, two months later the nine-year-old son of my wife's sister, our nephew Nathan, was diagnosed with a brain tumour. This turned out to be highly malignant, and unfortunately, he was called home to be with the Lord shortly after surgery. We can be sure of his destiny as shortly before his death little Nathan had testified to God's saving grace in his life.

My personal hopes for a long and cancer-free life appeared to be dashed on 25th July 2002. After several months of symptoms, I eventually conceded to having investigations. This included a colonoscopy and as a colorectal surgeon, I was accustomed to performing this test. Being on the receiving end however, was a different matter. I was given light sedation and was able to make the diagnosis of bowel cancer myself. To compound the issue I then had a CT scan, which revealed multiple tumour deposits in both lungs.

If ever I needed God, now was the time. Averil was unaware of the fact that I was having the test that morning. When she was called at home, being the astute person she is, she quickly came to the correct conclusion. The bottom had fallen out of our world. Both of us, the father and mother of our children, had developed cancer within the space of seven

months and the likelihood was that I would be
dead within the next year.

Naturally we were distraught, but on returning
home we turned to God's Word. Our text for
that day was Daniel 12:13; "But go thou thy
way till the end be: for thou shalt rest, and
stand in thy lot at the end of the days." More
precious to us than the verse itself was the title
in Spurgeon's notes: "Nothing to alarm us".
We were obviously very alarmed, but God was
offering the reassurance of His protection.

The next few days required lots of God's grace.
We had an appointment with the oncologist
and then had to travel to Castlederg where my parents
lived and to Carrickfergus to speak with Paul's mum and
dad. We wanted to break the news to them in person.

During Paul's surgery on that Friday morning friends
gathered for prayer at Limavady Baptist Church. I certainly
felt the benefit of these prayers and support while I waited
patiently at the hospital on Paul's return from theatre. We
were glad to hear that the surgery had gone well. The next
step was for Paul to undergo approximately nine months
of chemotherapy treatment.

Again Paul commented on his recollections of those days:

In Altnagelvin Hospital my operating list was
on Fridays. On Friday 2nd August 2002, I was
lying in my own operating theatre, my name

was on my own operating list as a patient rather than the operator, and I was having an operation that I had regularly carried out for others. This would be defined as a palliative procedure as I was, and still am, officially defined as being terminally ill.

The primary tumour could be removed, but the secondaries in the lungs would persist. Two friends, both of whom are Christians: my colleague, Robert Gilliland, and Keith Gardiner, a consultant from Belfast, operated on me. The Great Physician also played a part. This became particularly evident as, at one point, a stapling device failed, but thankfully this was quickly recognised. If not, I would probably have required a colostomy. This, I believe, was an answer to the prayers of God's people. Not only were my family praying for me, but also, our church, Limavady Baptist Church, had organised a special prayer meeting for the period I was in the operating theatre.

I was now on a conveyor belt, which at times felt more like a roller coaster with many ups and downs, both physically and emotionally. It was never a concern of mine as to why we should have been afflicted like this, but rather, it was my desire to know what God was going to achieve through it. I reckoned that if anything good was going to come out of this I would have to survive long enough to at least regain some degree of good health. I felt compelled to tell others of God's mercy, not only in saving me, but also by promising eternal life to anyone who simply puts their trust in Him.

I was aware of Christian stalwarts and men of God in the Scriptures who actually thanked God for the suffering they had experienced. I reckoned they must have been mad, but having already experienced something of 'the shadow of death' (Psalm 23:4) myself, I now recognise 'the peace of God which passeth all understanding' (Philippians 4:7).

As a direct result of what we have been through we have been blessed. It would not be true to say that life is now simply beautiful or like a bed of roses, but, if it were, there would have to be thorns, which can make life very painful at times. However, for those who have put their trust in Him we have many guarantees of God's provision for us. We have the reassurance that God is our refuge and strength in times of trouble and that, if we leave whatever is burdening us with Him, He will give us rest (Psalm 55:22 & Matthew 11:28).

As a family we continued to be sustained by knowing that many Christian people were remembering us in prayer. Numerous cards and letters of encouragement streamed steadily through our letterbox and these certainly heartened us

Chapter 12

The Last Lap

For almost nine months I accompanied Paul to the hospital for all his chemotherapy sessions. I remember that on several occasions a little letter or card would arrive just as we were leaving our home. These cards always seemed to have a very appropriate scripture verse to suit the circumstances of that day. While I was waiting at the hospital I would read over those verses again and draw help and strength from them.

Paul responded very well to these chemotherapy sessions. His stamina and strength increased with each succeeding round of chemotherapy. His lung metastases responded well to the treatment, and in between sessions he was able to return to his work and carried on with his operating lists and outpatient clinics. At the same time there were ups and downs during those months, but throughout the duration of his illness he maintained a good sense of humour. He often remarked to his patients that they were better off physically than he was. With this, he also took the opportunity to remind them that they needed to know for certain if they were going to heaven should they not waken up after their surgery.

I still smile when I remember the day Paul arranged for a gentleman from the bank to come to our home so that Paul could draw up his will.   I offered to stay and make coffee for the visitor, but Paul insisted that I go on to the shops. I did so and while I was gone the man duly arrived. I cannot remember how long the visitor stayed or how long I spent at the shops. When I got home Paul said to me, "Do you want a laugh?"

I sat down to have a cup of coffee while Paul told me his story: "The visit by the man from the bank went well, and I was able make a will. However, after I had finished our business, I left the banker to the door and waited to see him drive off. The poor man got embarrassed when he found that the car battery was flat. The result was I had to push his car down the park until the engine started and then he drove off in haste. I thought to myself, that's a good one, even though I'm the one who is dying, and yet I'm the mug who had to push the banker's car up the park."

Paul dealt with his illness in a dignified and private manner. He never gave up hope that God could heal him, if that had been His will. His outlook was always positive and was constantly encouraging the children and me to pray for a healing touch.

In January 2003 we were able to take a family holiday to Florida for three weeks. It was a great opportunity for the five of us to spend time together. We visited all the Disney Parks with the children, bathed in the sun and enjoyed eating out. It was a special time for us and a memorable holiday for the children.

By July 2003 a year had passed since Paul had first been diagnosed with cancer. He, therefore, began to consider alternative treatments for his illness. We were introduced to a rigorous juicing programme with a totally organic diet, a major part of which was to detoxify the body's system. Paul followed this strict regime while still continuing his prescribed medication. He started this therapy in September 2003. Our friend Mary Gilfillan was so kind and industrious to help us. Every day she came to our house and worked slavishly with me in the kitchen peeling carrots for juicing that same day. Sadly, the diet did not have the desired effects.

By the end of October 2003, he began to experience some cerebral symptoms and a subsequent brain scan confirmed what Paul had expected, metastases where now present in his brain. Even then, Paul remained positive. Matthew was ready to sit his 11+ examination in the hope of gaining entrance into a grammar school, and Paul was determined to help him do well.

Just after Christmas that year, Paul agreed to be admitted to Belvoir Park Hospital for some radiotherapy. While there, his condition deteriorated rapidly, and he was transferred to the Foyle Hospice.

During these weeks he was able to write a booklet, "At the Cutting Edge", in which he related his testimony and experience of God's help through his illness. His desire was that many would read this account and personally come to know his Saviour, Jesus Christ. Here are Paul's closing thoughts as he neared the end of his booklet:

At times I didn't know if I had any future left here on earth. Particularly, as a result of the complications associated with chemotherapy, I have often had the heartfelt desire to die. On many occasions I have thought, as my namesake, Paul the apostle, wrote, that it would be better to be with Christ (Philippians 1:23, 24). However, God has given me more time to continue my responsibilities as a husband and a father. He has allowed me to fulfil all of my goals to this point.

Initially I did not know if I would see Christmas 2002. I did, and not only that, I was able to go with our family on holiday to Florida in January 2003. This was despite having been discharged from hospital only two weeks previously, with major complications from chemotherapy.

I have also been able to see my daughter through her school transfer examination and into a new school. I am trusting that God will allow me to do the same for my son who is going through the same process this year.

Much more important than this, God has given me a ministry, which would otherwise not have happened. I have been able to return to work and be a help to my patients in a much more personal way than ever before. Having a worse medical condition than many of my patients, I am better able to address, not only their physical, but also, their emotional and spiritual needs. I have had several opportunities to discuss spiritual problems with members of the hospital staff and have been able to witness to God's grace at both local and national medical meetings. I know that many people have now heard my story and trust that God can use this to His glory.

It is my hope that my story will encourage you, if you are walking on your own, to earnestly seek after Christ. The Saviour told us in the Bible that those who seek Him will find Him; "And I say unto you, Ask, and it shall be given you; seek, and ye shall find; knock, and it shall be opened unto you" (Luke 11:9). The same Bible tells us that those who do not seek Him are fools who will ultimately be cast into the lake of fire; "And whosoever was not found written in the book of life was cast into the lake of fire" (Revelation 20:15).

One of the advantages of having cancer is that the patient often has time to prepare for eternity. Many people die suddenly or unexpectedly, and nobody knows when the Lord will return to take those who trust in Him to their reward in Heaven (John 14:3). The Old Testament prophet Isaiah instructed · us to seek the Lord while He may be found (Isaiah 55:6) and Paul warns us that now is the accepted time to make this decision for Christ (2 Corinthians 6:2).

Have you turned to God and asked for forgiveness of sin? Do you have the promise of eternal life? Not only that, but He has promised He will never leave you nor forsake you in this life, as well as in eternity.

I pray that you will answer God's call and that you find Him as your own and personal Saviour.

Unfortunately, for us, on the 15th February 2004, Paul passed away, very peacefully, into God's presence. Thanks to the attention of the staff at the hospice he never suffered any pain. Before he left us Paul penned his open letter:

Paul's Final Letter

Dear friends,

It is now near the end of January 2004, and I write from Foyle Hospice, which humanly speaking, this should be my last port of call.

I arrived here via a short stay at Belvoir Park Hospital, where I had some Radiotherapy. Although Brain Metastases (advanced secondaries) have now developed, I thank God that, though weak in body, I am lucid in mind and, reasonably so, in speech.

These past weeks have been an emotional rollercoaster, yet I have proved God's unfailing and loving presence. He has allowed me to see my young family saved and to learn that my story is being made known to a worldwide audience.

It is my prayer that it will be for His glory alone - and that many will come to know my Saviour through its challenge. Life is brief - It is time to seek the Lord, and there isn't necessarily time to prepare.

I know God can yet touch me in response to the earnest prayers of His people. However, he may wish to use me as a 'corn of wheat' (John 12:24).

Whatever, His will be done - I am content.

Yours In Christ,

Paul

Chapter 13

Friends Indeed

We were deeply indebted to our long-time family friend and previous pastor, Rev Tom Shaw, who frequently visited Paul and ministered to him and us throughout his time of sickness and our sorrow. He recalls those days:

After more than fifty years in pastoral ministry I have never become used to or hardened to meeting individuals or families in circumstances of great distress. I always find it quite painful and at times, upsetting to identify with these folk when they are up against tragedy or passing through heart-rending episodes of life.

I will never forget the day when I received a call from Averil Neilly to tell me that her husband, Paul, had been diagnosed with an advanced stage of cancer. It was even more ironic to learn that he had not only diagnosed himself, but his particular type of cancer was in the very area in which Paul was specialised to operate on others.

When I heard the news I left our home in Donaghy and travelled to Limavady to visit Paul and Averil. Although they were stunned, as were all of us on hearing this sad news, they also showed great composure and Christian fortitude in facing this circumstance that had suddenly been thrust upon them. Averil's concern was primarily for Paul while his was for the welfare of his wife and children.

We read the scriptures for their comfort and prayed for a miraculous intervention from God. That was not to be.

Thereafter, I made regular visits to their home or hospital and when I could not go, Mabel and I maintained contact by telephone, always holding them up in our prayers. In conversation with Paul during one of those visits he told me that he knew he was dying and his time was short. However, he further said that while he contemplated his pending demise he had two concerns; first, he wanted to die with dignity and in second place, he wanted his last days to glorify his Lord. I am glad to say that over the next eighteen months I witnessed these desires being overwhelmingly fulfilled as Paul slowly deteriorated and finally passed away.

It was painful to watch Paul's strength ebb away as the dreadful disease took its toll on his brain and body. This was especially true as we saw him confined to bed at the Foyle Hospice in Londonderry and then watch him slip into unconsciousness. His weakened and emaciated form was only a shadow of the vibrant young man I had known in earlier times.

Our prayers and compassion were very much with Averil and her young children as she watched and diligently attended to her husband right until the day the Lord took Paul home.

Paul Neilly truly fought a good fight and finished his course as a faithful Christian. It is not that his life was cut short. In God's plan his course was completed. He departed this life and went to be with Christ.

We thank God for every remembrance of Paul.

Although Averil's family lived at quite a distance from Limavady they were a tightly knit unit and supported each other through their times of sickness and tragedy. Averil's sister and brother-in-law, Linda and Tom Buchanan MLA, the parents of little Nathan who died in 2002 just a few months before Paul was diagnosed with his terminal illness, recalled their relationship with Paul and Averil.

Tom writes:

On our first meeting with Paul Neilly we found

him to be a quiet and shy individual. The first
impressions of this tall, slim and dark-haired
gentleman who was in training to be a
surgeon, endeared us to him and we knew
deep down that he was going to be a good
husband for Averil.

Paul had a strong faith in the Lord Jesus Christ
as his Saviour and held firm views in biblical
doctrine, church government and the covenant
established between God and man.

Paul had a humble spirit and for someone in
such a prominent position within the medical
field, he never boasted of his profession, but
always kept it in the background.

Paul's main interest and burden was to share
his personal faith in the Lord Jesus Christ and
to see others come to know Him as their
Saviour too. To have them turn from their sin
and enjoy that great assurance of Heaven at the
end of life's journey.

On being diagnosed with bowel cancer, Paul
bore his trial with great fortitude and patience.
He had a peace in his heart because he had the
assurance that all was well with his soul for
eternity and when God's call might come, for
him it would be absent from the body to be
present with the Lord.

While death held no fear for Paul, yet as a husband and father he was greatly burdened for Averil's and the children's future and daily covenanted them to the Lord in prayer.

Paul Neilly was also a friend and brother in Christ to us when he helped us in our time of severe personal trial. While we miss him on our pilgrim walk we know we will meet our beloved brother one day in heaven.

'So until then my heart will go on singing, until the day God calls me home'

Linda added her appreciation for her brother-in-law and Averil when she remembered how they received the news of Paul's home-call.

Linda wrote:

We were so happy for Paul when he took up his post in Altnagelvin and saw his family well settled in Limavady.

In early 2001, Tom and I met Paul in the corridors of Altnagelvin one morning. We later remarked that he must have been under pressure with work and long hours as he looked pale and tired. Little did we realise the sore trial that Paul, Averil and the children were soon to face.

When we visited with Paul, Averil and the children, both at home and in Foyle Hospice, the circumstances were so difficult.

Our hearts were heavy on leaving them, yet we did indeed sense the presence of the Lord as a refuge and strength and a very present help in trouble.

On the Lord's Day morning, 15th February 2004, we got the sad call from Averil to say that Paul's time was slipping away. Finding the news very hard to take in we immediately made our way over to mum's house.

It was such a bright sunny morning when we left home, but as we made our way down into the Derg Valley, the mist was so intense it was difficult to see. Not long afterwards we received another phone call from Averil to say that Paul had gone home to be with the Lord. At that moment we knew without a shadow of doubt that Paul was indeed in glory. The fair and sweet morning had dawned for him and he was in Immanuel's land.

Norman Somerville, an elder at Limavady Baptist Church, was a great support for our family through Paul's illness and the months that followed his death. He had his own recollections of Paul and the Neilly family:

The Rev Jim Neilly was the young minister of

Tobermore Presbyterian Church in Co. Londonderry in the early 1960's. With my pastor at that time, R. A. Boggs, of the Baptist Church there, they had formed 1st Tobermore Company of the Boys Brigade. Mr Neilly was Captain, and part of his leadership included teaching the Bible Class each Sunday afternoon. As his first young staff sergeant, I was privileged to get to know him well and appreciate his teaching. Little did I know that one day, over forty years later, that teaching in the Word of God would help me to minister to his own consultant surgeon son, at a time of great need and deep trauma in his life.

Paul Neilly, MD, FRCS, with his wife Averil and three young children, came to Limavady Baptist Church in 2001, following Paul's appointment as Consultant Surgeon at Altnagelvin Hospital, Londonderry. Just one year later Paul diagnosed himself with bowel cancer. With the courage we came to associate with him, he wrote his widely read little booklet, 'At the Cutting Edge', and having got to know him well, I interviewed him on our church radio station, New Life Radio, at Easter 2003.

Late one night, towards the end of the year, Averil's quiet voice came on the telephone: 'Norman, could you possibly come round? Paul would like to talk to you'.

The disease had begun to take a stranglehold. In the subdued light of his bedroom, I found an anxious and unsettled Paul in what might be called 'a dark night of the soul' frame of mind. Paul was considerably distressed in trying to accept the enormity of the fact that it seemed be God's will to take him home to heaven. However, this distress was not for himself. He had an overriding concern because he felt he was failing to fulfil his responsibility to his beloved Averil and his young family - leaving them to cope on their own, as well as the natural hurt that he would not be around to see the children grow up and bring a dad's help to their lives and expectations.

The Lord gave me Psalm 28: 6-8 to share with Paul, 'The Lord is my strength and my shield... he is the saving strength of his anointed'. Paul's anxiety turned to a heaven-sent peace as he accepted by faith the Lord's promise; 'You are Mine, I purchased you with My blood, and in taking you, your family is My responsibility too, when they commit their way unto Me'. The peace that the Lord gave him that night remained with Paul through his final days.

Though his brain was heavily infected with the disease, his mind remained lucid and he was able to give his medical colleagues 'cutting edge' advice within a few days of his death. I last saw Paul the day before he died early in

2004. He was serene and at peace. For sure, he had an abundant entrance into the presence of the Lord he loved and served so faithfully. It was an immense privilege to know him and have some meaningful part in his life.

I am also so grateful to the Lord that, as a church elder, I was able to visit Averil regularly after Paul's passing, and to talk and pray with her and the family, as she took things 'a day at a time'. Naturally anxious and feeling overwhelmed at the beginning, gradually she learned to trust the Lord completely for all things, both the big and the small issues. It was very moving when she shared how she had 'angrily had it out with the Lord' over seemingly unanswered prayer for Paul's healing – and when she had her say, how He gave her an immediate and overwhelming sense of His peace that drained all bitterness, replacing it with His assuring presence, that has remained with her through all the ups and downs, highs and lows of their family life.

Bringing up her family, Hannah, Matthew and Samuel, without Paul by her side, and guiding them as best she could, has been testing as they each dealt with their grief in their own way. However, they are lovely young people and are a credit to Averil - and to Paul, who set the early course of their lives on the right path, one that honoured God and His Word.

It is no surprise that the Lord has given to Averil a widespread ministry of testifying and sharing her experience of how the Lord enabled her to cope with grief. God has gifted Averil with a voice which conveys sincerity, gentleness, the love of the Lord Jesus and a unique experience to share with others of God's grace to help in time of need as they face their challenging circumstances.

May the Lord be pleased to bless Averil's future ministry and that of 'Beyond the Cutting Edge'.

The children and I did appreciate all the ministry of God's servants. However, I was now left without my husband while Hannah, Matthew and Samuel had lost their daddy. Like me, they loved their dad so much.

Chapter 14

What is God's Answer?

During Paul's illness and many times since, I have pondered the age-old question, "Why did God not heal my husband?" In my weaker moments I used to reflect on what might have been if I had only prayed more effectually. Or, as in the case of Moses, if only there had been a man who was able to stand in the gap, perhaps God would then have answered prayer and spared Paul. I must confess that there were times when such thoughts caused me a lot of concern.

When we talk to some people who earnestly maintain that God answers prayer by miraculously healing all Christians from all their illnesses then we are confronted with some difficult questions about healing and why our God did not allow our Christian loved ones to recover from their sicknesses.

One day while Paul was still undergoing his treatment, I received a phone call from an individual who asked if I would send him a handkerchief or something belonging to Paul as he and his friends wanted to pray over the article for Paul's healing. Apparently, the same man had earlier offered to come to our home and pray with my sick husband, but Paul did not accept the man's offer. I also declined to accede to the man's request to send an article of Paul's clothing.

Some time after Paul's death someone from the same group of people contacted me to ask how Paul was. When the person heard of Paul's death, I detected a tone of disappointment in his voice that I had not allowed God to work through their prayers while Paul was still alive.

At the same time, Paul did invite the elders from Limavady Baptist Church to come to our home and lay their hands on him, anoint him with oil and pray for his healing. Their prayers were earnest and sincere as were ours. So much prayer went up to God on Paul's behalf. People and churches all over our country and beyond had special times of intercession for him. Did God answer those prayers? Yes, but God in His sovereignty did not answer in the way that we would have desired, but as He saw best. His way is always perfect, and He makes our way perfect (Psalm 18:30, 32).

This book is not the place nor am I the person to try to examine all the mystery of suffering in relation to our faith in God. However, there are some things I have had to bear in mind. Being a Christian does not shield us from suffering or eliminate us from death and sorrow. It is true that Christians are born again people, but we still remain human and are touched with all the weaknesses of our human frame. We still feel pain, bruise and bleed when we are cut. We do not invite sicknesses or welcome any sickness, but we are exposed and often subject to the common maladies which touch society in general. At the same time we also recognize that God is wholly sovereign, and has His plan for our individual lives. I have found that His plan is always better than ours.

Perhaps the most notable book in the scriptures to deal with suffering, sorrow and death is one of the Bible's oldest books, the book of Job. In this book, which bears his name, we read of this godly man of God who suffered unimaginable tragedy with the death of his sons, the loss of his property, his fortune and his produce. On top of it all he then lost his health. The forty-two chapters of Job do not provide us with an answer to the mystery of sorrow and suffering, but they do set out the truth that God is sovereign in our lives and in all our circumstances. It was the awareness of this that caused Job to bow before God and confess, "Naked came I out of my mother's womb, and naked shall I return thither: the Lord gave, and the Lord hath taken away; blessed be the name of the Lord" (Job 1:21).

Furthermore, in the New Testament we understand that the great Apostle Paul was no stranger to physical weakness and suffering. In 2 Corinthians, the most personal of all his letters, he frequently alluded to his human frailty and ongoing suffering. In 2 Corinthians 12 he referred to his suffering, whatever the cause or nature of that condition, as "a thorn in the flesh". The apostle went on to say that he prayed repeatedly that God would heal him from that malady and remove that thorn. As was the case with our prayers for my husband Paul, God did answer the apostle's prayer, but not in the way he had repeatedly requested. Instead of healing, God gave him sufficient grace, in place of removing his thorn, God sustained him with divine strength for the apostle's weakness.

Over a long period of time and through many tears, I have painfully learned to accept God's sovereignty in all my circumstances. I began to see that when the Lord did not allow me to escape from my suffering and sorrow, He gave me sufficient grace to help me endure those difficult circumstances. He did not restore Paul to us, but He sustained me when I was so vulnerable and weak.

Having come through the most difficult years of my life I now find that the Lord has also enabled me to employ my experience so that I am now able to help and comfort others in their sorrow and complexities. God did not grant us the miracle we desired for Paul's healing, but He did help me to be able to cope with our loss and teach me lessons, which I trust will benefit others.

In recent years God has given me the opportunity to speak at various churches and women's groups where I have been able to share with many people of how God has helped me to handle my dark days of grief and also testify of God's sufficient grace in these adverse circumstances. On numerous occasions after these sessions, grieving people, often with tears, have approached me to share their own heartaches and seek help and counsel in their sorrow. Some of these bereaved individuals have lost their spouse, their parents or even a son or a daughter. Every case is different and I have found that every individual approaches bereavement in a different way. I frequently find it difficult to hold back the tears as I listen, but at the same time, without having passed through my own years of sorrow I would not be able to help, comfort and encourage these folk.

Another outcome of my experience of grief and loss is that God has used those many tears that I shed to wash my eyes and help me see the better and more lasting values of life.

I often feel hurt when Christians measure God's blessings by what they have and own. I must confess what hurts me most of all is that I used to think that way also. In earlier times you might have heard me say, "God has blessed us with so much. We have a lovely home, our cars and everything we need."

It was only when God began to take some of these things away from us and until I was left with just Jesus that God opened my eyes to the more important treasures of life. I was awakened to the empty values and false estimation I used to put on material things, the things I thought made our lives prosperous and successful. I used to lie in bed at night and think of how hollow my life had been by clinging to these temporal and paltry toys, which we had thought made us feel so blessed. I repented before God for being so shallow in my thinking and hollow in life's values, even though I professed to be a child of God.

In readjusting to this new reality I began to see the richness of those more meaningful, but often neglected attitudes and actions in my Christian life. Thereafter, I made it a deliberate exercise to thank God at the end of each day for every blessing I had enjoyed during that day: the visit of friend who had called by our home, the opportunity to invite a lonely person for a coffee in town, the enjoyment of driving alone while listening to inspirational hymns of praise in the car, being able to visit a lonely or hurting person in their home or at hospital, receiving a verbal thank you or hug from my children or writing a letter to a friend. For me these were priceless. I tried to fill each day with significant deeds of kindness, which not only blessed others, but me also.

Most of all, I learned to be even more thankful that I am saved and that my husband, Paul, is with the Lord. I live with the assurance that we will all meet again.

God did not give me answers. He gave me and gives me grace for each day.

Chapter 15

Samuel Makes Me Smile

The Lord does send us encouragements along the way and sometimes they come from the most unexpected sources. I have always been aware of, and at times overwhelmed by, the awesome responsibility I have as a single parent to raise three lively children, all of who have a mind of their own. At the same time I am really amazed and on many occasions very blessed to see how God turned the tables and used the same three children to teach, encourage and allow me to praise God for what He has done in their lives.

My children are my treasure. Samuel was the most mischievous of our three children, yet when he smiles at me I find it very difficult to chastise him. He was only eight years old when his dad died. A friend told me recently that on the Sunday afternoon, after I had told Samuel about his dad's death, he went round to her home to play with her son, Aaron. When he arrived in their house he announced, "My Dad has just gone to Heaven."

It has been difficult for me to see Samuel excel in sport, namely rugby, knowing that Paul would have been so proud of him. Instead of his father's encouragement, over this past two years poor Samuel has had to suffer the humiliation and indignation of hearing his mum screaming and shouting from the sidelines of Ravenhill Rugby Stadium while he carried or chased the oval ball up and down the field.

Of course, as a mother I am immensely proud of all our three children when they achieve their different goals or milestones. At the same time, I inevitably shed tears when I think of what Paul has missed.

Just recently I came upon an article Samuel had written as a school exercise in which he summed up his appreciation of his mum. I was a little embarrassed but greatly blessed:

> My mum! More to the point, what do I not admire about her? She is the most helpful, supportive and relaxed mum. I say relaxed because by the type of person I am, I don't know how she does it.
>
> To me she is known as 'my mum' but to you she would be known as Averil Neilly. She has a family of four, including herself. She is over the age of twenty, well, that's what she tells me anyway and she works in a clothes shop.
>
> First of all, why do I admire her? I admire her because to me she is everything. Without her I would have nothing. Every morning she wakes me up and every night she says good night, but

that is only the start of it. From when I was born to the age I am now she hasn't stopped looking after me when I am sick or well. She never leaves my side. When I am down and sad she'll make me feel happy. That's what mums are for. I admire her because she is only one person and one person only. She will treat me the same when I am by myself and she will treat me the same when I am with other people. I watch her when she is with other people. I get a sense of joy, happiness and pride because I think to myself, that is my mum.

I used to always think to myself, why does she always have to be angry at me? But now, when I look back I thank her for being like that. I now look up to her, for in my eyes she is perfect. I want to be like her because of who she is and not who she pretends to be. She treats everyone like she would treat herself.

My mum, Averil Neilly, is a gem in my crown. Without her I would be missing something, but with her I am perfected. Again, I admire her because when I need something she will help me out, even if she can't do it herself. I don't know what I would do without her.

My dad, her husband, died a few years ago. I have never seen someone stay so strong. I know that if I was in her situation I would be close to giving up, but she was like a brick wall, which didn't let anything knock her down. I want to be like that, so that is why I admire her more than anyone else.

I am sure by reading this you may have realised that I do admire my mum. She may look angry sometimes when I arrive from school with a bad note, but I am sure that deep down she still loves me. Does anyone not admire his or her mum? 'Cause, if you don't, I'm worried.

Samuel is my youngest son and watching his development has been like watching an unfolding story. I wish his dad had been around to see how God answered our early prayers for our baby.

Chapter 16

Hallelujah for Hannah

I was again greatly helped at Ballycraigy Congregational Church when I asked Rev Tom Shaw what his thoughts were on young children being saved. I related to him how that on one recent morning our four-year-old Hannah announced to me that she had asked Jesus into her heart during the night. When I asked how this happened she told me that she had awoken after a very bad dream and was very scared that she could die and not be ready to meet God.

Tom was most encouraging and said not to disregard what she had said. Every morning I shared a devotional reading and prayer with the children, and I could see that Hannah was always learning from this short time together.

Once I was praying for an unsaved member of our family she asked me again if that person was not already a Christian. When I answered in the negative, she replied, "Don't you think you had better go talk to him?"

Hannah was and still is my little challenger. One night we were returning to the car following tea at Pizza Hut. I guess she would have been about three or four years old at that time. As I lifted her to put her in her car seat, I noticed the car beside me waiting to move off, so I hurriedly dropped Hannah into the seat and then closed the car door over to allow the other car to move off first. When I opened the door to secure her into the seat, Hannah had a little scowl on her face and said, "Did you have to pour me into my seat?"

When Hannah started Limavady Central Primary School shortly after our arrival in the town, she witnessed to a girl in her class about becoming a Christian. Later on at lunch time the two girls huddled under a coat, wanting to have their heads covered while Hannah prayed with her classmate. The mother of the girl phoned later that evening to tell me how thrilled she was about her little girl. I was astounded for Hannah said nothing about it at home.

Following New York's infamous 9/11 incident, which was widely reported around the world, Hannah began to have doubts about her salvation. One night near bedtime and following the tragedy, we were all together in the living room. Hannah did not seem to be at her usual perky self. She quietly wished us goodnight and went on up to bed. I mentioned to Paul about my concern for Hannah, but he reassured me she would be fine.

Fifteen minutes later I decided I would go to her bedroom just to check that she was ok. I was glad I did for I found she was weeping into her pillow over her lack of assurance of her salvation. I asked if I should call dad, but she said that she wanted me to talk with her and then pray for her.

I gladly complied as she had requested and after praying, left with her a little verse which said "All that the father gives me shall come to me and he that comes to me I shall in no wise cast out" (John 6:37). Many years later I noticed that Hannah had copied that same verse unto a piece of paper and had written the date beside it, "the date on which Mummy prayed with me."

Hannah is now exhibiting much spiritual fruit in her Christian life and has grown into a beautiful Christian girl. She spontaneously spends much time in reading and studying the scriptures and has had the opportunity to attend several Christian camps in North Carolina, USA, and has been on two mission trips to Morocco.

She has also been a great encouragement to me, especially over these last three years. We talk freely now of our feelings about her dad's death. I think that was something which would have been too difficult to touch on in the years immediately following Paul's home going.

Hannah is currently studying in Preston, England. She recalls how she tried to cope with her grief and living through her teenage years without her dad's guidance and counsel:

> I will never forget the nights spent in bed pleading to God not to let my dad go. I knew that my dad's life was in His hand, but also I knew that God listened to my prayers and that maybe dad would be miraculously healed. He's been gone now for ten years, and I can honestly say that I wouldn't change one thing. God does

answer prayer; He has provided and blessed me more than I could ever ask. Even though the Lord has taken away a fifth of our family, He has blessed us ten times more, and just like it says on Dad's gravestone, "The LORD gave, and the LORD hath taken away; blessed be the name of the LORD" (JOB 1:21).

I had a great upbringing with two godly parents who truly loved God and loved each other. There is nothing more that a child could ask for than that. I'm so thankful for parents who know how to respond to the request, "I need to get saved." That is what I said to mum at my bedside in September 2001. She was able to lead me to personal faith in the Lord Jesus. I always saw myself as a daddy's girl, and I have many fond memories of him as my hard working but fun-loving Dad. Whether he was trying to pull out one of my wobbly teeth or calling me square-eyes because I was constantly watching the television, I knew without a doubt that I was loved beyond measure.

I had a really hard time showing my emotions when Dad was diagnosed with cancer. While I felt that I had to be the strong one, I would cry anywhere and everywhere as long as no one could see me. I used to cry a lot in church because I felt everyone would be looking at the pastor. I will always remember singing the chorus "Jesus, All For Jesus". I used to stop singing, and then the tears started falling from my face into my hymn book, but there was one voice beside me that never faltered. It was my dad's. I could hear him clearly singing, "All of my ambitions, hopes and plans, I surrender these into your hands." It really touched me to know that even though Dad was going through these unimaginable circumstances, yet he was able to sing these words with such conviction.

After many months in which he put up a very brave fight, dad left this earth and even though I could have been so mad at God, I felt complete peace. I knew that he was no longer in pain, and although his departure had left a great hole in my heart, God immediately poured His love into my heart and my life, like only a Heavenly Father could.

I was a miserable teenager to live with. I gave my mum such a hard time and now I would do anything to turn back the clock to put that right. On occasions I stopped all communication with my mum, and I spent most of my time in my room. On the outside I still appeared a sweet, Christian girl, but my heart had strayed far from God. I spent many years in this confused and mixed up state. I knew I was saved but was not having any personal relationship with Jesus Christ.

It wasn't until 2007 when I met a missionary couple and their four children who had come to work at the Roe Valley Baptist Church in

Limavady, I could see the relationship the girls had with their parents, and I just wanted to be part of their family. I started to spend more and more time with them, acting like one person when I was with them, but a totally different person when I got back home. However, I started to make some changes on the outside. I began to pay attention to how I dressed, what I watched on television and how I spoke. I had cleaned up my life externally, but I still had not made a change in my heart. On the following year I attended a Bible Camp in United States of America with that missionary family. While there I met many young Christian girls with sweet and godly attitudes. I so wanted to be like them. Slowly I started to change. I spent more time in my Bible and in prayer and that started my way back to God and a personal relationship with Him.

The real test came in late 2008 when the missionary family decided to leave Limavady and return to the United States for good. I knew this was my chance to see if I was spiritually mature enough to stand on my own two feet. I had gotten most of the basics. Another missionary family came from the USA and started working in the same church in Limavady. They were a young family and I was able to spend a lot of time with the pastor's wife. She gave me discipleship classes where I got to know my Bible better and became more grounded in my Christian faith.

In 2009, after trying to convince God that He was wrong, I finally surrendered to His calling to become a missionary. I was listening to a preacher via the internet and he mentioned that we are always in God's hand and wherever we go, He is with us. During that service I physically felt God's hand on my shoulder, and I knew that He was speaking to me. I still don't know where He wants me to go, but He is leading me every step of the way.

Even though there had been a change in my heart, I still could not remove the barrier I had built between my mum and me. I had such a desire to be closer to her, but my stubbornness and pride would never let me get over my unreasonable anger. I think God knew it was going to take something big in my life to help me overcome this hurdle. I went off to Switzerland on my gap year before starting university. The culture shock and homesickness I felt while there was so intense that I was completely broken. I called home to my mum every day, and for the first few weeks I cried my eyes out while talking to her. At home I had never let my mum see me when I was crying. I always felt it was a sign of weakness. Now on the phone from Switzerland I told my mum every day that I loved her. God had taken this piece of clay, mashed it and started recreating a new person. After my bitter experience, my advice to anyone who has a broken relationship with their parents is that they need to get down off their pedestal and open up to their parents. Let go of all the anger and hatred they might have in their hearts and let God start forming this new person in His image.

Now as I look back over this last ten-year journey that I have come through, there is only one thing that I can say, "God has been faithful." And I know that He will continue to be faithful. He has completely healed my relationship with my mum, and I can honestly say that I have never been happier. All my burdens have been lifted.

I am currently in England studying TESOL (Teaching English to Speakers of Other Languages) and French, with Spanish and Arabic. God has been with me every step of the way as I prepare to serve Him. I have given God complete control of my life, and I am so excited to see what He will do with it. He is continuing to mould me into the person He wants me to be, and I can say with confidence, "He who began a good work in me will be faithful to complete it" (Philippians 1:6).

Hannah Neilly

Chapter 17

Meet Matthew

During the early years of our bereavement on many occasions, I went to bed deeply distressed and anxious about some incident that had occurred with the children that day. It might have involved a lack of communication where something was said in anger, which caused deep hurt on their part and consequently, great isolation on mine. When these situations occurred, as they frequently did, the children left me alone downstairs while they went up to their rooms. How I now wish that I could have dealt better with my grief than I did.

All of us were hurting, but we did not realise it. We inflicted stinging wounds on each other with our words or lack of them. On nights like these, all I could do was cry and pray. Sometimes I was in the depths of despair and often wondered if the children, given a choice, would have preferred that I had died and their dad lived.

In the months that followed his daddy's death Matthew struggled to accept the changes in our home, but at the same time he endeavoured to be my protector. I always felt that he wanted to look after me in his daddy's absence, undoubtedly, trying to fulfill the role of the man in our home. In contrast to Hannah and Samuel, Matthew was more vocal about his feelings and better able to express to others how he felt.

Matthew surrendered his life to the Lord one night following a Holiday Bible Club in our church. It was so good for Paul to know that all of our children had trusted the Lord before he passed away. I remember a difficult time in Matthew's school life after his dad died. He arrived home from school very distressed because someone had been bullying him. He told me that night that he could not go back to school again. I was very concerned for him and was not able to get over to sleep. Throughout that night I frequently checked in on Matthew to see if he was ok, but I was so distressed for him that that I finally ended up on my knees in the middle of a freezing cold night. I cried to the Lord and pleaded for Matthew's well-being and happiness in school. I felt that God would have to intervene, for I was totally inadequate. At the same time, it seemed that I could not get through to God with my cries. Eventually, I rose from my knees, my body felt as though it was frozen. I fell back into bed, totally spent from crying, and eventually fell asleep.

When morning dawned Matthew had breakfast and went off to school as usual. However, I kept him before the Lord all through that day. I apprehensively picked him up that afternoon when school had finished and was pleasantly surprised to find him to be quite content. I was frightened to ask how his day had gone seeing he seemed to be so happy. Not being able to contain the suspense any longer, I nervously asked Matthew, "Well, how did today go?"

"Mum," he answered, "Someone must have given that boy a new heart, because he never bothered with me today and has now started bullying someone else."

I lifted my heart to God and thanked Him for answered prayer. I also took time to pray for the bully and his other potential victims.

Matthew has been a real encouragement quite recently when a young man in our church fell seriously ill. Without any prompting from me Matthew called a time of prayer in our home to pray for this young friend. What encouraged me most in this was that in spite of God not giving our children the answer they wanted when we prayed for their dad, yet they still believed in the benefit of intercessory prayer on behalf of others.

Matthew has always been protective, caring and wholly responsible as the older of my two boys. He kindly gave his own account of how he has responded through these years of grief:

> A verse that I don't remember learning, but have always relied on is; "And the Lord, he it is that doth go before thee; he will be with thee, he will not fail thee, neither forsake thee: fear not, neither be dismayed" (Deuteronomy 31:8). After losing my earthly father, I've had to rely on my Heavenly Father so much more. This verse has been tried and tested, and God has never failed me. At times I have questioned

Him, but He's an all-knowing God, and I fully trust Him. His ways are perfect.

I'm sure you have gathered so far how I have been blessed with such an amazing father and mother. Growing up in a loving and Christian home, being taken to Church, Sunday School, Children's Meetings and being taught from the family Bible during our devotions, these have given me the fundamentals of my beliefs and strength from day to day. I sincerely thank them for spending their time in teaching us, guiding us and loving us in every possible way.

The year 2002 proved to be a very difficult year for our family. Nathan, my cousin nine days younger than me, was diagnosed with a brain tumour and was taken to heaven in May of that year. I couldn't understand why God would take my closest friend at that time. Nathan and I were inseparable. I can remember being at the wake in his house when his teacher, Rosemary King, was there. I immediately bonded with her that night and didn't leave her side. I told Rosemary how sad I was and she spent time talking to me, and I thank her for that. She wanted me to go into the room where Nathan was and I refused to go as I knew Nathan was in heaven and not lying in a box. After this, I became very close with auntie Linda, Nathan's mum. I felt that I could relate to her and almost wanted to be a Nathan to her. I remember not long after Nathan died I came into their house the dogs were barking and Linda said that she thought the dogs were thinking that was Nathan coming back home. I found it so easy to talk with Linda and even share things with her that I couldn't share with my own mum. I questioned God through this time, but just had to accept it for I knew I would see Nathan again someday.

On that same summer of 2002 dad was diagnosed with bowel cancer. At the age of nine, I honestly didn't know what cancer was. I knew he was sick, but my parents, being the loving people they are, tried their hardest to let me stay a kid as long as the situation would allow. When my dad got really sick, I did and said a lot of stupid things. Everyone does silly things at times like this because in the midst of all that pain and fear, it's difficult to be the best possible version of yourself. I wish someone would have told me to go a bit easier on myself for not being able to figure it all out when I was in the middle of that situation. The truth is that there is no guidebook, no set standard for how to go through the experience of losing someone you love. Every situation brings its own set of challenges and emotions. For me there was no right or wrong way of grieving. I wasn't sure if I was crying enough or crying too much, or if I needed to grow up and be the 'man' in our house.

Shortly after this, I remember John McCormick

asking me to have a talk with him because both my brother and sister were Christians, and I needed to become one. I knew I needed to do this and make this decision, but I didn't want to just yet. It did happen one night after our Holiday Bible Club at Church. I came home from the church that night and went straight to bed where I asked God to save me. I knew I wanted to see Nathan again, and if anything were to happen to my dad, I wanted to be with Him in heaven someday also. I simply told God I was so sorry for everything I had done wrong, and asked Him for help to live right and for Him to save my soul. I thank Him for His new mercies every single day.

Dad was admitted to the Foyle Hospice when he began to deteriorate. I remember the first day going to see him there and walking into his room. When I saw him I fainted. I told them it wasn't my dad lying there. For me Saturday 14th February 2004 was an exciting and beautiful day. I had received my 11+ results in the post that morning, and I remember sitting in the car the whole way over to the Hospice with the results unopened on my knee. I wanted to open them with dad. I remember when we got there I jumped on his frail knee and saw the big smile on his face when we opened the envelope. I had passed. He told me he loved me and was proud of me. This was the last day I saw and hugged my daddy.

Days, months and years passed, without a father figure in my life. When I was moving through Grammar School it started to dawn on me how much I was going to have to do in life without my dad being there. People say time eases pain. This is true, but it doesn't remove the pain. But God gives grace and strength for each day. There still are days when I miss my dad more than on other days, but there's never a day goes by that I don't think about him, or remember something he has taught me. Memories are so precious.

Growing up through secondary school was also difficult, but I was glad I still had a loving mum and home to come home to each evening. I thank God for both Christian and non-Christian friends that surrounded me in these years and helped me through the days when I was really struggling. When it came to sixth year in school I was struggling quite a lot so I made the decision that school wasn't for me. I left school when I was seventeen years old. I believe this was all in God's plan for me because I knew I would have struggled with trying to keep in the straight and narrow way. I went on to study at Greenmount Agricultural & Horticultural College and got greatly involved in Christian Union there. While at Greenmount I met a great group of Christian friends.

I have made some great friends in my life and

have a fantastic group of friends at this present time. The majority of these are Christians and walking with the Saviour. I thank them for their encouragement, love and friendship. If you're grieving, struggling or just need a listening ear, talk with someone. I have found that by sharing my grief with someone who cares really helped me immensely and lifted the burden off my own heart.

There are many things in life I do regret doing, but God doesn't love us any less for these things. He wants to draw you closer to Him. I continually thank Him every day for sticking close to me, when I have been down deep in the valley and when I have been singing on the mountaintop.

I write so many things down in my Bible. We attended a Youth Weekend where I scribbled down a list which I keep reading over and over again.

Ten things God wants You to remember

1. I will revive you
2. I will strengthen you
3. I will answer you
4. I believe in you
5. I will bless you
6. I am for you
7. I will not fail you

8. I will provide for you
9. I will be with you
10. I love you

Growing up was difficult for all of us. But, all these things have happened for a reason. Everything has been in God's will, and the reason why may be unfurled to us some day. I remember finding and listening to a CD from dad's car which he loved. It is titled, "Thank You" by Ray Boltz. I love one of the verses and chorus;

> *One by one they came,*
> *Far as your eyes could see,*
> *Each life somehow touched*
> *By your generosity.*
> *Little things that you had done,*
> *Sacrifices you made,*
> *They were unnoticed on the earth,*
> *In heaven now proclaimed*
>
> *And I know that up in heaven*
> *You're not supposed to cry,*
> *But I am almost sure*
> *There were tears in your eyes*
> *As Jesus took your hand.*
> *And you stood before the Lord*
> *He said, 'My child look around you*
> *For great is your reward.'*
>
> *Thank you for giving to the Lord.*
> *I am a life that was changed.*

Thank you for giving to the Lord.
I am so glad you gave.

I'm excited for what God has in the future for
me. My ultimate aim is to please God and to
be His willing follower. I love working with
children and young people and being involved
in church work. I want to show everyone their
need for the Lord and help them in whatever
way I possibly can. People need the Lord. I
want to place all things before Him and make
my Heavenly and Earthly Father proud.

"God whispers to us in our pleasures, speaks
in our conscience, but He shouts in our pain.
It is His megaphone to rouse a deaf world." C.
S. Lewis

In reading these brief tributes by my children, all I can say
is that they will probably never know how much I love
them. They are my life and my constant and earnest prayer
is that they will surrender their lives to God's will and
grow to love and serve Him all of their days.

Chapter 18

How Dark is Your Valley?

I remember coming home that afternoon to tell the children that their dad was now in heaven. The saddest thing for me was that I loved them so much, yet I could not protect them from the cruelty of death or make this awful situation any easier as I felt a mum should be able to do.

As I said before, the days that followed were a bit of a blur, and I do not recall much about the funeral other than that the church was packed to capacity.

In the days and weeks that followed Paul's death and funeral the children and I had to cope with big adjustments. While family and friends were always on hand to comfort and help, at the same time, I was grateful that they gave us space to grieve and come to terms with the circumstances that had been thrust upon us. This enforced change was not easy, not for me and certainly not for the children. I greatly missed my husband, and while the children missed their father, I missed the guidance and the authority of a father figure in the home. At times when I would try to correct some misdemeanour or guide them through some problem they would retort, "If daddy was here he would not have done that," or "I miss daddy, for he would have been able to help me." These remarks were crushing.

When I was going through the throes of trying to cope with various pressures and conflicting emotions I wondered how a person who is not a Christian would be able to deal with these strains and trials without having Jesus Christ in their lives. Even in my darkest moments I was able to reach out and cry to the Lord for His help and comfort. Psalm 46 reminded me that He is never absent from us in our trials; "God is our refuge and strength, a very present help in trouble. Therefore, will not we fear, though the earth be removed, and though the mountains be carried into the midst of the sea" (Psalm 46:1). When our world seems to be falling apart God assures us that we need not be afraid. I not only found that God was never absent from me in my troubles, He was always adequate for and in control of every situation.

I was greatly comforted in the Psalms, the central book of the Bible. I almost felt that as I read the various Psalms they, in fact, were reading me; they met me just where I was, and I was able to identify with so much of what the psalmist had written. This was especially true when I came to the well-known Psalm 23. For years I had read and even memorized this Psalm, but now in the aftermath of my loss and sorrow I found that Psalm 23 took on a new significance for me. Perhaps when we look at this Psalm through our tears we see things that dry eyes cannot perceive.

The words of Psalm 23:4 were especially helpful: "Yea though I walk through the valley of the shadow of death, I will fear no evil, for thou art with me, thy rod and thy staff they comfort me." It is for that reason that I now use this verse when speaking to people about their valley of grief. One of the first things to understand about grief is that it is not wrong or sinful to grieve. The Bible records at least three occasions when the Lord Jesus Christ grieved. The Prophet Isaiah referred to Him as the One who was the "Man of sorrows and acquainted with grief" (Isaiah 53:3). Furthermore, Paul, the apostle wrote to the Thessalonians that although Christians grieve it is not without hope (1 Thessalonians 4:13).

As I mulled over this verse I realised that when we come to the valley of the shadow of death we have no option but to enter, even though it is the most painful valley we have ever faced. We have no other choice. We cannot flee from it or turn back to more pleasant pastures. However, if we know Christ is with us, we can enter this valley of the shadow with our fearful hand in His nail-pierced hand and then lean upon Him.

I had entered this valley through no choice of my own. God had not given me an option or the opportunity to turn around and go back. This valley was my lot.

Entering the valley was without choice, but enduring the valley was another matter. I discovered I had to make a choice. At times in the early days of my grief I harboured bitterness and resentment. At other times, I experienced a strange and incomprehensible peace by resting and accepting that which I could not change. While I vacillated between these two emotions I came to the conclusion that I would have to choose between one or the other, either to maintain that resentment or to accept God's plan for my life and that of my children. I longed for the peace of acceptance, but, at the same time, I realised I could not do this in my own strength. I needed Christ to go before me and at the same time be beside me. I am thankful that God gave me the grace to be able to choose His peace, a peace which passes all understanding.

It is true that this dark valley is full of fear. But I was comforted by the words of the Belfast-born author and Christian academic, C. S. Lewis, who wrote a book on grief after his wife, Joy, succumbed to cancer. He observed, "I wish someone had told me that grief is so much like fear, that dry mouth, the constant swallowing and nervous feeling in one's stomach."

For most of those days I felt that I was enshrouded by this terrible fear. It was as if I was being pursued by an enemy and could not shake him off. I feared for the future without Paul; I feared that the children would not be able to cope without him; I worried constantly about what might happen if I became ill again, and I was fearful about facing the rest of my life as a single woman. In relation to this, I painfully discovered how difficult it is for widows or widowers to find social acceptance after they have lost their spouse. This can happen as easily within a church family as much as in the secular society. In my darker moments when I was gripped with this anxiety, I feared that God had abandoned me and did not really care for me or for my children. It was a dreadful feeling. I tried to flee from the awful thought of God deserting us, but try as I might, it seemed to plague me. It was in those sombre and dark days that I needed to read again God's firm and faithful promises by which He assured us that He will never leave nor forsake us.

I found loneliness in the valley of the shadow was the most crushing emotion of all. I had my children at home, which was such a blessing, but I yearned and pined for Paul and for his love. In my darkest nights I felt like pleading with God to let him return, even if it was just for one night. I knew this was ridiculous, but I also knew that if this absurd request had been granted I would not have let Paul leave this life without me again. Sometimes the pining for my husband became so severe that I almost felt as though his presence was still with us in our home. I could visualise Paul in every room. Throughout all these illusory emotions all I could do was to bare my wounds of grief and in my tears, carry my burden to the Lord and ask Him to heal my broken heart and life.

I also felt that I had lost my identity. I had always been known and often referred to as "Mr Neilly's wife", or "Mrs Paul Neilly". Who was I now? I was still married and continued to wear my wedding ring, but, oh, how I hated to be introduced as, "This is Mr Neilly's widow.

With widowhood also came the loss of friends. I missed the camaraderie of Paul's professional colleagues and their spouses and involvement with his other acquaintances. Once those work ties were broken most of the associated friendships became fragmented and soon disappeared. I found this to be very difficult then and still do today. Even now when we invite friends to our home for a meal I miss

Paul not being there to be part of the conversation. My valley was so dark.

At times when I was left alone I racked my mind and cried from my heart to the Lord, "Why me Lord? Is it because I haven't served or loved You as I ought? And why did You not answer the prayers for Paul's healing? I hear of others who have been healed from cancer, and I almost feel resentment. I do not think I will ever be able to pray as before or ask You for anything again."

The fact that I could not see or hear God in my suffering meant that this was one of the darkest episodes of my valley. Those despairing days in the valley were full of shadows and dark hours. What I did not realise was that where there is a shadow, there has to be a light. God was that light, and He was still with me, but I could not feel His presence.

When I reflected again on Psalm 23 I began to see some comfort and hope that I had not seen before, and most certainly, not when I was first crushed with grief.

First of all, I realised that the psalmist tells me that God enters the valley with me. He said, "Thou art with me." For that reason God was telling me not to fear, His rod and staff would provide protection and direction for future days.

How thankful I was to also be reminded that a valley not only has an entrance, it also has an exit. It is not a dead end cul-de-sac. We may have to go through the valley of grief, but there is an end to that valley, and when we emerge out on the other side, God wipes away our tears so that we are able to view again the majestic mountains of splendour all around us.

Further observation of this Shepherd's Psalm taught me we do not rush through the valley. We walk, we must not try to rush or speed up the grieving process. It takes time. I had to walk with my hand in His, for He had promised to be at my side, never to leave me or forsake me.

Isaiah 30:21 promises, "And thine ears shall hear a word behind thee, saying, This is the way, walk ye in it, when ye turn to the right hand, and when ye turn to the left." My immediate concern after Paul's death was about the future: how would I cope, and what would happen to the children. I tried to look into the future, but that was futile.

When I was engrossed in my grief I could not see what lay ahead in this valley. At times, I still questioned God as to why we had to go into such a difficult valley, but there were no answers. We cannot see the way ahead, the path before me was too winding and the way too dark to understand what was going to happen in a week's time or for a month ahead. I really only began to be able to cope with these imponderables when I learned that as Christian's, we walk by faith and not by sight.

The Bible says this faith is "...the substance of things hoped for, the evidence of things not seen" (Hebrews 11:1). That means that faith acts upon the invisible as if it were visible and real and anticipates the future as if it were the present.

Chapter 19

Grace for the Grief

Back in 1969, Swiss-born Dr Elisabeth Kübler-Ross provided a very helpful "Grief Cycle" in her seminal book, On Death & Dying. In it she explained the process of dying and described her now classically regarded "Five Stages of Grief". The book, and the supporting publication of her ideas in Time magazine, achieved wide circulation, so that Elisabeth Kübler-Ross soon became known for her pioneering work with the terminally ill and for her ideas in the counselling and support of those affected by death and bereavement.

Her findings have been used as a text book for many counselors all over the world. However, her methods in developing and defining her ideas have also been subject to some debate and criticism. I recognize that the topic of mortality, including our reactions to death, attracts serious and passionate interest and may be understood, rationalized and 'treated' in many ways.

For that reason I think it should be said that Dr Kübler-Ross's ideas and her "Five Stages of Grief" should not be taken as an absolute or wholly reliable scientific concept. Death, as life itself, means different things to different people. Therefore, remember that these stages may not be so clearly defined in an individual's experience and may often merge, overlap or even be repeated.

I suggest you do what I did: take from her findings what you find to be helpful, and encourage others to treat this information in the same spirit.

Dr Kübler-Ross's cycle of grief and healing generally passes through these stages:

1. **Denial.** Denial is a conscious or unconscious refusal to accept facts, information, reality, etc., relating to the situation concerned. It's a defence mechanism and perfectly natural. Some people can become locked in this stage when dealing with a traumatic change that can be ignored. Death of course is not particularly easy to avoid or evade indefinitely.

2. **Anger.** Anger can manifest in different ways. People dealing with emotional upset can be angry with themselves, and/or with others, especially those close to them. Knowing this helps us keep detached and non-judgemental when experiencing the anger of someone who is very upset.

3. **Bargaining.** Traditionally the bargaining stage for people facing death can involve attempting to bargain with whatever God the person believes in. People facing less serious trauma can bargain or seek to

negotiate a compromise. For example "Can we still be friends?" when facing a break-up. Bargaining rarely provides a sustainable solution, especially if it's a matter of life or death.

4. **Depression.** Also referred to as preparatory grieving. In a way it's the dress rehearsal or the practice run for the 'aftermath' although this stage means different things depending on whom it involves. It's a sort of acceptance with emotional attachment. It's natural to feel sadness and regret, fear, uncertainty, etc. It shows that the person has at least begun to accept the reality.

5. **Acceptance.** Again this stage definitely varies according to the person's situation, although broadly it is an indication that there is some emotional detachment and objectivity. People dying can enter this stage a long time before the people they leave behind, who must necessarily pass through their own individual stages of dealing with the grief.

Our vision is so limited that we can hardly conceive that our heavenly Father's love would not protect us from suffering. We must remember that the love of the Father did not protect His own Son. He will not, therefore, necessarily protect us from anything it may take to make us more like His Son. The hammer, the chisel and the flame often are used in the process of the Father's plans for us.

When my husband died I could not change it. I could not change the fact that I was a widow, nor that Paul was gone and my children were left without a father. The only thing I could learn to do, was to accept it.

Acceptance did not come easily. It never does. I grieved deeply, as anyone else would grieve. I had fallen in love with Paul. For twelve years we had built our lives together. God had blessed us with three wonderful children. Now it was over. I had to realise that God had assigned this as my portion in life.

In acceptance I had to learn to lift up my empty hands and say: "Lord, I don't understand why this has happened. I most certainly would never have asked for it. I do not have the answers to the whys, but I have learned so much from Your Word. You are the Sovereign and only wise God. By Your grace, I accept what you have done and submit my life to your ways."

It took a long time for me to surrender my heart, mind and will to come to this place, but unconditional acceptance to His will is the best way to peace.

While on my journey through grief and sorrow I have had to cope with widowhood and becoming a single mum. The adjustments and slow process through my experience of sorrow was not easy, at times very frustrating, and it still is. However, sometime ago I read a few suggestions, which really helped me through those difficult and frustrating days. I am not sure where I read them, and I may well be guilty of plagiarism. Nevertheless, they helped me and I would like to pass them on for your benefit, or even for you to be able to help others who may be going through a similar grieving process.

1. Talk – Allow the bereaved person room and time for talking.

Allowing the grieving individual to talk is very important. Let them converse freely until they have no more to say. This may often mean for you to be a silent listener and content to be quiet. It is important to refrain from talking about your own experiences of grief or making glib statements like, "I know how you feel." We often do not really how they feel. Better to patiently listen and nod your head in agreement as appropriate.

Allow the grieving one to speak about the person they have lost, even when this is accompanied with tears. Recounting some memories or stories you can recall about their deceased loved one will often cheer the mourner and bring some comfort. When we lose a beloved family member we often worry that he or she may be forgotten. Talking about them is one way of keeping that memory alive, and that is comforting.

Of course, the best talking is that which is directed to God in prayer. Often in stress and grief it is hard for a person to pray. That is why God has placed us into "His body". Every part of that body should support the other and we do that when we pray with and for those who grieve. Best of all, the Lord Jesus also intercedes for us.

2. Tears – do not be ashamed of tears.

We should never be frightened by tears, our own or the tears of others.   Weeping plays an important part in expressing our sorrow and can often relieve us from our built up emotions.

If the grieving one weeps, sometimes clasping their hand or offering a tissue can be helpful.   Never suggest that the person should stop crying or tell him or her that the departed loved one would want them to be brave and not cry.

Our tears are also important to the Lord.   Psalm 56:8 assures us that the Lord keeps all our tears in a bottle, and that they are written in His book. Personally, I found tears to be a healing agent and perhaps for that reason they are made up of salt and water, common commodities used for the cleansing and healing of wounds.

3. Touch – the gentle touch or shake of the hand can communicate immense sympathy.

This can be as little as a hand on someone's arm when asking how he or she is doing, or even with appropriate people, it might be a loving hug. Usually we can judge from a person's body language what they are comfortable with.

4. Time – Grieving is a process which should not be rushed.

As mentioned earlier, everyone moves through the valley of grief at a different pace.

No two people grieve exactly the same or on the same time scale. The loss of a parent differs greatly from the loss of a child, just as the loss of a spouse is a very personal grief. In no way though, should any type of loss be compared to another. Grief is very individual and unpredictable, and it is hard to catalogue it into defined stages. I have heard people suggest that on the death of an elderly relative a person should not grieve so much since the loved one was elderly or had been very ill for such a long time. Such a statement may have been intended to be helpful, but can be very hurtful to the grieving one. Try to avoid glib or pat answers to people who are hurting. There are no quick fixes for these situations. We need to ask for the help and guidance of the Holy Spirit as we seek to comfort others.

Grief may not come to a screeching halt, but it does get easier with time. Someone has likened grief to a jagged stone which we constantly carry in our heart. Initially, we feel the darting pain of its rough edges. However, with the process of time our heavy hearts smooth off those sharp and rugged edges and just leave a tedious weight. The stone will always be there, but because the rough edges have gone, the sorrow is not just as painful but still gives us a heavy heart.

Give the mourner the necessary time to grieve as much as they need to. There may be circumstances where a person becomes "trapped" in their grief and not able to move forward or make any progress. Such a person may need professional help.

5. Tokens – Try to be practical when seeking to help the bereaved.

The Bible says, "But to do good and to communicate forget not" (Hebrews 13:16). How true is this advice. A little practical kindness can be a great encouragement to those people who are passing through their valley of grief. This is often referred to as practical Christianity. It is important to pray for our bereaved friends, but we show that we really care when we put feet to our prayers.

Practical Christianity may involve organising a rota where a few friends are prepared to provide meals, shop for groceries or go on errands. To receive an unexpected casserole or pot of soup can be a great blessing and brighten a dark hour.

Chapter 20

Helpful Tokens

I remember one day when several people came to visit me and they were still visiting with me when the children arrived home from school at 3.30 pm. An hour later my visitors had not yet gone home, and I could see the children, obviously feeling a little peckish, make periodic and plundering visits to the kitchen. I was becoming a little frustrated as I had nothing prepared for dinner and these friends were slow to leave. I was so greatly relieved when another friend arrived at the door with a cottage pie, which was still hot and ready to be served. This friend did not know that she was an angel sent by God – in the nick of time, her name was Rachel.

This angel's name was Rachel, and she often visited us with a little pie or something for the freezer. Thank God for good friends like Rachel who was a constant and caring friend.

One of the first gifts I received in the days immediately following Paul's funeral was a journal. This encouraged me to pour out my deepest thoughts, funnel them through a pen on to paper and fill the journal every night. Months later I was able to look back over those writings and see how I was progressing. I remembered that immediately after Paul's death I had recorded how I cried every morning after waking and again each night as I went to sleep. I then noticed that three months later I had recorded in the journal that I was only crying once each day and was able to give thanks to the Lord for a friend who had come by to take me out to visit a lovely garden centre and then for a coffee or lunch.

A month after Paul died the children bought me a teddy bear for Mother's Day. I not only appreciated and was touched by this expression of their love and kindness, but was also struck by their instinct and sensitivity. That teddy bear became the most hugged and cried into teddy bear that ever had been made. There were many nights when sleep would not come. I just cuddled teddy close to me, and when I cried he soaked up my tears. Thank you Hannah, Matthew and Samuel for such a caring gift.

For those who record dates, thoughts and their experiences in a daily journal, I suggest you make a note of the date of your friend's bereavement. After that highlight the thresholds that person will cross over the next year: six weeks since the bereavement, three months, six months and the first anniversary. Plan to send a suitable card or pay a visit to them with a plant or flowers on these dates. By so doing you will reassure that person that you are still remembering them and do care for them.

It is helpful to offer transport and company to the grieving party when attending various functions at church, school or other functions and events. I found this to be very helpful also, especially going to various parents' evenings at school. I did not find it easy to enter alone into a room or hall filled with people, most of whom I did not know. It was helpful, although still daunting, to enter the room even with someone accompanying me.

There are many other thoughtful ways by which we can help and comfort our grieving friends. You may want to remember their birthday or their wedding anniversary by sending a little gift or flowers.

Sometimes, Christian women are not sure how they may be useful in serving God. I think comforting the bereaved is a very special area of service in which they can be very valuable. It takes only a few minutes to write a card and a little longer to cook a meal.

God has commanded us to comfort and help others if we have been comforted in the past: "Who comforteth us in all our trials, that we may be able to comfort them which are in any trouble, by the comfort wherewith we ourselves are comforted of God" (1 Corinthians1:4). I also found that the best way to break the habit of worry is to develop the habit of praying. I think the apostle Paul had this in mind when he wrote, "Be careful for nothing; but in everything by prayer and supplication with thanksgiving let your requests be made known unto God" (Philippians 4:6).

Overcoming grief demands that we look out beyond ourselves, begin to look up to God and look outward on the needs of others. Furthermore, we must try to look beyond our grief and see what lies ahead for us.

We can only harbour two emotions at any one time. Either we can nurse our bitterness and resentment or choose acceptance of that which you cannot change. A choice must be deliberately and consciously made. I am glad that I chose acceptance.

Looking back over the grieving process I can see that it was necessary, but at the same time, I must confess that it was painful, complicated and at times, very hard work. However, recognising and allowing time for each stage of that process was important and an essential part of healing my broken heart.

Going back to Dr Elisabeth Kübler-Ross's book, On Death and Dying, she made a comment that I think is so very true: "It's only when we truly know and understand that we have a limited time on earth - and that we have no way of knowing when our time is up, we will then begin to live each day to the fullest, as if it was the only one we had."

I could not have gone through these years without the Lord by my side, and I have proved that His grace is sufficient. Grief, which at first seemed to be my enemy, by His grace, became God's instrument for my emotional healing.

There is joy beyond the cutting edge.

Postscript

I was blessed and greatly helped by having such a good family around me. Paul's parents faithfully came to visit us every two weeks and stayed overnight. That must not have been easy for them, but it was great for the children and me. Their interest, prayers and support for the children have been a great encouragement.

My cousin Lorraine Finlayson married Martin Monteith, her one and only love. They eventually moved to Barrie, Ontario, Canada. In the summer of 2004, shortly after Paul died, Lorraine invited the children and me to spend three weeks with them in Canada. Hannah, Matthew and Samuel had a great time. I did too, but I missed Paul so much.

My mum too has been so caring. She had to carry the added burden of caring for her sister and for our dad through his illness until he went home to be with the Lord in 2006. I remember thinking one day that the two favourite men in my life were now together in heaven. Despite all the difficulties my mother faced she still managed to find time to come and spend a night or two with us.

Other family members have also been a big encouragement to us. We are grateful to Paul's brother Stephen and his wife, Anne, for keeping us in their prayers. Likewise also, to my sisters Linda and Elaine and their respective husbands, Tommy and Samuel, for their practical help. They were always on hand when one or another of our home appliances was not working or when something needed to be repaired. My brother Stephen and his wife, Averil, were also quick to visit us in Limavady and engaged in some DIY jobs. When I remember these helpers I recall the saying, "A friend in need is a friend indeed."

The children and I had two wonderful summer holidays with Paul's brother, Mark, his wife, Hazel, and their daughter Rebekah. They also kindly opened their home and let us spend our first few Christmas Days with their family while we adjusted to that festive and family season without Paul.

Unfortunately, we did not have a pastor at Limavady Baptist Church when Paul was diagnosed. I was very grateful that one of our elders, Norman Somerville, was faithful in visiting our home to read and pray with us after Paul's death as did Pastor Jim Smyth, our former pastor, when he was able. These pastoral visits helped to guide me through some of the darkest days.

Satan tried to destroy our family and our testimony, but

he has not been able to do so, and by God's help; as far as I am concerned, he never will. God is at the root of our family and our lives. It is the Lord Who has kept us standing firm. I suppose it is true to say that what the devil meant for evil God has used for our good and for His glory. God has made this evident to us by allowing me to minister to so many broken people that otherwise I would never have encountered. I am reminded of Isaiah 55:9; "For as the heavens are higher than the earth, so are my ways higher than your ways, and my thoughts than your thoughts." No matter what the anguish and pain may come into our lives we can be confident that the Lord can give us beauty for ashes. That is the reason why I have written this book.

What a wonderful prospect heaven is. So many of our loved ones have already gone there and now they are watching and waiting for us. It may sound strange, but now, when I sit by the bedside of a dying saint, I want to ask them to find my husband Paul in heaven and tell him we are doing ok.

I am grateful for those who pray for Hannah, Matthew and Samuel. They have all put their trust in the Lord. I earnestly pray that they will continue to live for Christ and serve the Saviour as their dad would have wanted them to do. It has not been an easy road for them. Each one has grieved very differently. They are so very precious to me and I love them dearly.

My sincere thanks goes to all who have prayed for me over these years. God has answered these prayers and the very fact that I was able to write this book to testify of God's amazing grace and constant faithfulness is an abundant evidence of this.

Thank you,

Averil Neilly